MW01520372

Our Redeemer – Husband: Our Head

Patricia has written a very clear and succinct presentation of headship, which has become a very misunderstood and misaligned function in our world and in the church today.

She shares a revelation of headship that I believe is representative of God's heart for Christ's body. She presents three levels of headship that bring heaven to earth, which when in proper alignment, allow the very Life of God in our lives and fellowships. As she so aptly puts it, "Headship is the supernatural life-flow that brings God's presence to earth and establishes all authority, and power to fulfill His purposes here." In this day and this hour this is a very timely message that we need to hear and experience.

Phil Lichty
Overseer of Tree of Life/Arbre de Vie Church Family
and of Christian Mission and Training Commission.
Monetville, ON., Canada

I found this book to be thought-provoking. It challenged my view points by the fresh perspective of ministry that it presents. It motivated me to preach a sermon on the Body of Christ. I have appreciated the book, because it did cause me to think differently. I would encourage you to get this work published, as it will help many. Even though it might bother some readers, I believe this insight is of God.

Eugene Weaver
Gospel Crusade Ministerial Fellowship, President
Stevens, PA., U.S.A.

Our Redeemer-Husband: Our Head

Our Redeemer-Husband; Our Head

Patricia A. Hughes

Maranatha Apostolic Ministries, PO Box 731, Station B, Sudbury, ON., P3E 4R6, Canada

Printed in the United States of America

Publishing services by Selah Publishing Group, LLC, Tennessee. The views expressed or implied in this work do not necessarily reflect those of Selah Publishing Group.

ISBN: 978-1-58930-249-5
Library of Congress Control Number: 2010900745

Cover Painting by Rik Berry

ACKNOWLEDGEMENTS

There are so many to thank who have made this book possible.

First of all, I am very grateful to God who has birthed this undertaking and engaged many people (parts of His Body) to help in the process.

Some of whom I wish to honor and thank are:

My friend and associate Jean Fulin, who has paid a high price to fulfill her part, especially in some of the editing work.

My faithful team, who have prayed this book from conception into fruition, and loved me in the process.

Dennis Wiedrick, who has given apostolic encouragement and exhortation from the beginning.

Jim & Faith Chosa, for so freely sharing Kingdom Light and Love.

Daina Doucet, who became the editor/artisan in refining the form and metal of the work.

I am grateful for each person who read, encouraged and served as a prayer warrior along the way.

I am grateful to all those through the years: the speakers, preachers, authors, discussers, debaters, "commenters", friends and enemies, who have been my teachers.

CONTENTS

FOREWORD
BY DENNIS WIEDRICK

Every generation faces its unique challenges. Massive change seems to come reeling towards us at warp speed. In all areas of life we see major paradigms radically shifting.   *How do we as Christians cope with this?*

Does the church have a role in times like these?

Is there no voice that can cry out in the midst of the wind and the waves, "Peace, be still!"?

Thank God! I believe there is! And his name is Jesus -- Our Redeemer-Husband. Paul said, "For I know whom I have believed and am persuaded that He is able to keep that which I have committed to Him against that day."

There is no room for hopelessness, no cause for despair, no reason to fail! Our Redeemer has overcome, and as long as we are rightly aligned with Him - our Head, we have nothing to fear. We also read that "everything that can be shaken will be shaken so that only that which cannot be shaken will remain".

Jesus has laid the foundation of an unshakeable kingdom. And now we all, individually and corporately, get to build our lives, our homes, and our futures on that "Rock".

But why do we see so little evidence of victory in many believers' lives? Why are so many churches just surviving in "maintenance mode"? How many generations will pass before we actually complete the Great Commission?

These issues and more are addressed in this well-written book by Patricia Hughes. She is not afraid to ask the hard questions, nor is she timid about confronting some of our worn-out traditions that hinder our fruitfulness.

It is practically impossible these days to turn on the television without coming across numerous "home improvement" shows.

Every possible angle seemingly has been covered. The general premises of these programs go something like this:

> Sincere homeowners are anxious to sell their home at a good price. But for some reason there are no offers. So the design team comes in to the rescue, and with a very small budget, a little bit of paint and a few days of work, they "transform" a fixer-upper into someone's "dream" home. Then happily, buyers come along, fall in love with the house, and the sellers pocket the profits.

Not a bad plan, considering how often it works. But this is not the way God does things in the Body of Christ! Man looks at the outward appearance, but God looks at the heart. Man throws on a coat of paint, hangs a few pictures, and rearranges the furniture, and considers the house renovated! But God wants to take down the old paneling and look beneath the surface at the structure, the frame, and above all, the foundation of the building.

Herein lies the strength of this book. Patricia looks behind the surface layers of issues that many Christian books may address -- past the outward appearance, and gets to the heart of the matter -- our relationship with Christ as Redeemer, Husband, and Head. Only when we are in vital relationship with Him can we expect His life to be fully manifest in us. Only when we are in compliance with the original blueprint can we expect the approval of the building inspector - the Holy Spirit. And only then will we be given the permit to continue building.

I would encourage you to read this book thoughtfully and prayerfully. Let God's plumb-line reveal the quality of your workmanship in order that it always reflect His image. Examine yourself individually, relationally and corporately, and when you see that you are becoming rightly connected to Him, then go out and change the world!

Chapter 1

WHO IS THE REAL HEAD

OF THE CHURCH?

While attending an annual gathering of church leaders, I listened to a pastor teach on the art of shepherding. He worked in both vocations and had personally learned how the jobs of pastoring and shepherding were similar. Because this analogy is very biblical I was interested in his practical insight. I was not disappointed as he began to unfold what he had learned.

He made many interesting points concerning the behavior and habits of sheep, goats, wolves, sheep-dogs, and shepherds. Most of his insights and ideas were very good and could be helpful to pastoral people in doing their work with more wisdom. He delivered his material with humor and personal stories, which added to the value of his message.

At one point he shifted from a general comparison of pastoring and shepherding to assigning specific roles and responsibilities to church leaders and members, aligning them with familiar aspects of shepherding sheep. He assigned the primary shepherd's role to the senior pastor, the secondary role of sheep-dogs to elders, and the role of sheep to the congregation. His inferences caught my attention as he enlarged on the role of the senior pastor as the primary shepherd. He blatantly stated all "sheep" (congregation) and all "sheep-dogs" (elders) were to have total allegiance and be in total submission to the senior shepherd-pastor. In order to emphasize his point, he circulated a picture of himself as shepherd with his flock and dogs entirely focused on him. He maintained that the picture demonstrated how elders and congregation should relate to their senior pastor.

Although the concept of total submission and allegiance to a senior pastor may sound logical and harmonious, it is a dangerous deviation from the Church's total allegiance and submission to her Head, Christ. Jesus made this very clear in His teachings that we are to have total allegiance to only one Master:

> But you, do not be called 'Rabbi'; for One is your Teacher (NIV, one Master), the Christ, and you are all brethren. Do not call anyone on earth your father; for One is your Father, He who is in heaven. And do not be called teachers; for One is your Teacher, the Christ. But he who is greatest among you shall be your servant. And whoever exalts himself will be humbled, and he who humbles himself will be exalted (Matthew 23:8-12,NKJV).

> But Jesus called them to Himself and said, "You know that the rulers of the Gentiles lord it over them, and those who are great exercise authority over them. Yet it shall not be so among you; but whoever desires to become great among you, let him be your servant. And whoever desires to be first among you, let him be your slave, just as the Son of Man did not come to be served, but to serve, and to give His life a ransom for many (Matthew 20:25-28, NKJV).

Are we as church leaders truly the Head Shepherd, or are we one of the sheep (brethren) called to *assist the* Head Shepherd? I believe Christ says that we leaders are supposed to be part of the foundation of the Church, and servants of all, not masters. The primary question is, do we honor Christ as the Head of His Church in the fullness of God's divine intention, or are we deceived into *thinking* we honor Him, while we operate in or under human headship? We easily say, *Christ is our Head*, but how much of that is just a precept and how much is a living reality?

God has been talking to me about this subject for some time now, and it has become my reason for writing this book. A revelation has been imparted that exposes a primary obstacle for the local church – a deception of the beguiler – that has hindered the Church for centuries. This deception has deeply infiltrated the Church and distorted her glorious destiny in her beloved Head – Christ. This deception involves a substitution of earthly headship for Christ's divine headship in the Church and hinges upon lies that have obviously hindered God's Kingdom family business and His preparation of the Bride for His Son. God has decreed that the Bride of Christ will be without spot or wrinkle, and therefore it must be so. It is time to deal with this issue because the glorious day of our heavenly Bridegroom's return is drawing near.

The revelation of the substitution of human headship in the Church for the headship of Christ came to me after many years of searching and longing for the release of divine supernatural life as described in the Bible. Most of my church experience, as good as it was, didn't demonstrate the fullness of the supernatural life experienced by the early Church. In recent times my frustration and grief especially escalated when I observed the lack of spiritual life among the majority of men with whom I interacted in our region. For quite a season it became my personal prayer burden. Then a husband and wife team came from the Family Foundations ministry to facilitate a seminar in our city dealing with generational blessings and curses. After the seminar the husband shared a concern with me: his perception of the poor spiritual condition of the local men. In response I opened my heart and shared my prayer burden and a vision I had experienced during a time of prayer.

In the vision I saw two rows of men suspended on a type of rack, facing each other. A distance similar to a major highway separated them. Their feet were just off the ground, their heads hung down, and their hands were tied behind them. They looked despondent and shamed. At a distance was a large corral filled with women milling about. They were deceived into thinking they were free, but the men were not. As they moved around talking, some of them mocked the men for their imprisonment and added to their shame. Then I heard the hoof beats of a rider approaching from a distance. As I listened to this sound, I knew in my heart that his purpose was to set the men free. I also realized that the enemy was afraid of the men gaining their freedom because of the warrior anointing they would have. The biblical example of Jehu came to mind. The men would be warriors like Jehu whom God anointed King in a time of great national trouble, and to whom He gave the mandate to destroy wicked Queen Jezebel in 2 Kings 9.

When I shared this with the seminar facilitator, we both felt God drawing us into prayer. That prayer time together created the atmosphere for me to receive the revelation from God that I am about to share. I do so with some fear and trepidation, mainly because of the awe and fear of God I have experienced as He spoke to me about these things.

As you travel with me through the journey of exposing this deception and of sharing the insights that I believe God has given to me, I will introduce and explore several related issues that concern the Church and discuss how the problem of deception affects all aspects of our Christian lives and of the life of the Church. We will examine:

a) The effect of perception and traditions on understanding and communication within the Church
and their contribution to our acceptance of this
deception.
b) The comparison of the Church Body to some of the
biblical analogies, like that of a family business, an
army, and the human body.
c) Godly headship as it operates in its three primary
levels, especially on its initiation level with Christ.
d) Our struggle with understanding biblical concepts
due to our Greek mindset and philosophical ori-
entation as opposed to a Hebraic heart-centered
life-view.
e) Healthy and unhealthy aspects of body-life including corporateness verses individualism, and
symptoms of "disease" along with their "diagnoses."
f) God's design for the way men and women relate
within marriage and within the Church context to
achieve God's Kingdom purposes.

There can be a vast difference between what God means
when He speaks of Christ's Body, His Church and what we refer
to when we speak of the Church Body, as we know it. God has
spoken through various analogies and pictures to help us grasp
what He is talking about. Some of these images include an
army (see Ephesians 6), a city (see Revelation 21), a body (see
Colossians 1), a vineyard (see John 15), a Bride (see Revelation
21), an olive tree (see Romans 11), and a family business (see
Matthew 21), to name just a few. It is obvious that His ideas
and vision for His Church are vast and multifaceted.

We will begin by exploring a parable in Matthew's Gospel
about God's Kingdom, in the context of a family business. In

Matthew 21: 33-45, Jesus tells a story of a landowner, who planted a vineyard. He completed all the planting and building, and then leased it to others. When the time came to collect his profit, the tenants turned on him, on his servants and even on his son.

In this parable God reveals His heart and His plans. He started His family business expansion on earth in a garden with two stewards. He got it all ready and leased it to them. Their rebellion was similar to that of the prodigal son (see Luke 15:11-32) who insisted, *"I'll do it myself"*. They forfeited their lease to a usurper and robber who did not have God's interest at heart. Although the stewardship of the vineyard had been leased through a family covenant, the occupants wrongly acted like independent owners.

Like all good fathers, God has not quit, but is using the adversary to further His plans. He is working on something really important: a glorious inheritance for His beloved Son, which includes a very special Bride for Him. He knew that it would not be easy to expand His Kingdom on earth, and was well prepared for the battle.

As His plans unfolded, He chose certain individuals, along with their wives and families, to further their development – people like Noah, Abram, and Moses. From these individuals, He commissioned a people group called the Jews to walk with Him. He divided them into tribes and placed them in a garden called Israel. They also had trouble being faithful stewards over the garden that they were given stewardship of, through covenant. They compromised it with foreign gods, although they were clearly directed not to, and thereby dishonored Him. He had to discipline them repeatedly, but would also creatively use their situation to further His expansion plans.

God has long-term plans that have taken many, many generations to fulfill. A great number of them are still in process. He is completing a strategy that He, the Godhead, envisioned before creation began. His family vision is that of generations of His children – those born of the Spirit through the Blood of Christ – living in loving relationship with Him (Father, Son, and Spirit), and with one another. Only then can His plan to display His Kingdom to this world through the Body of Christ, be complete. As God's Kingdom is increasingly manifest on the earth in that manner, then God's words to Adam, "subdue the earth" will be fulfilled. The Bible says that the earth groans waiting for the manifestation of the Sons of God. This earthly Kingdom family must reveal to the people of all nations that He is the true *Father,* and that Jesus is the true *Son.* Then the earth will also respond with joy.

In the Old Testament God's family plan was established through the twelve tribes of Israel. Now, the family plan is exhibited through the Body of Christ in every nation of the world, including modern day Israel with her prophetic destiny. Each generation of faithful sons and daughters that walks in obedience to Him is a responsible steward of our God's Kingdom purposes here on earth, because the purpose of the family business is to establish the Kingdom of God on and in the earth.

To ensure that our heavenly Father's long-term generational plan continues to be developed, those before us, and now we, must respectively demonstrate that we lovingly honor His sovereign ownership of everything in Heaven and on the earth. We must keep our ear tuned to His heart while in loving fellowship with Him. That's the only way we can know His divine purpose from season to season and generation to generation.

The Old Testament reveals how God's family has functioned throughout the generations until the coming of Christ. It highlights examples of faithful children such as Gideon, who did incredible exploits. It also gives examples of those who lost faith in God and failed miserably – men like Saul, who became consumed with fear and pride. God our Father has been transparent in His Word about these successes and failures so we can learn from them and not repeat the same mistakes. Part of our family heritage is the generational blessing of not having to keep starting over again, but of walking on the "shoulders" of our fathers and mothers in the faith.

With the coming of the Messiah promised to Israel, God implemented the ultimate expansion plan! The family lineage took on another dimension. God sent His Son – a divine visitation – to earth. It resulted in young Mary becoming pregnant with the God-man, Yeshua, by Holy Spirit. God Himself is the Father, Christ the Messiah is the Son, and Israel, through Mary, is the mother of this new supernatural family unit. The wonder of wonders is a living, divine Son, here on earth. God has birthed a clean man – the Son / Adam – to undo what the original Adam did, and to bring His Kingdom rulership back to earth.

For someone to become a member of God's family covenant and business plan, requires much more from us today than it did before Christ came. Previously it was primarily a matter of natural birth into a Jewish family line and obedience to the law given to Moses. But now, with the coming of the Christ, family membership moves into a deeper and costlier level. Through His crucifixion and resurrection we are redeemed and invited into a higher covenant with Him – the supernatural "birthing" or impartation of God's own divine life taking up residence within us: His rulership and ownership of us! It is an exchange of lives: His life for ours; ours for His. This is a "beachhead," we might say, of God's own divine presence in us for the purpose of co-eternal life, here on earth. In this way we are made one in, through and with Him, as Jesus' prayed in John 17:22, 23.

Each of us is therefore a beachhead wherein Heaven and earth connects so that Heaven can invade earth wherever we are. Through this union of God and man, God's purpose for man to occupy earth and fulfill His business mandate can be accomplished. We become the extension of His Son's kingly rulership here: stewards and ambassadors for Him.

Our Kingdom position is about warfare. Jesus said "Do not think that I came to bring peace on earth. I did not come to bring peace but a sword. For I have come to 'set a man against his father, a daughter against her mother, and a daughter-in-law against her mother-in-law'; and 'a man's enemies will be those of his own household.' He who loves father or mother more than Me is not worthy of Me. And he who loves son or daughter more than Me is not worthy of Me. And he who does not take his cross and follow after Me is not worthy of Me. He who finds his life will lose it, and he who loses his life for My sake will find it" (*Matthew 10:34-39, NKJV*).

This is "military talk" that speaks of God's army. This army is to co-operate in the establishment of many beachheads and in taking back the ground that was usurped by the enemy.

Chapter 2

ESTABLISHING KINGDOM BEACHHEADS

A few years ago a military-minded colleague strongly encouraged me to watch a war movie. Normally viewing violent movies is abhorrent to me, but I did want to see what his purpose was. The movie was entitled *Saving Private Ryan*, but Private Ryan's story was not my homework. The establishment of a beachhead was to be the visual lesson which was graphically displayed at the beginning of the movie. It portrayed the World War II D. Day invasion of Normandy and the landing of Allied troops on the Omaha Beach on June 6, 1944.

The horror of war was well woven into the replay of that morning when the troops were ferried into position to land on an uncovered beach in full sight of enemy guns overhead on the cliffs. I had never thought of what that would be like and it stirred me deeply. The barges landed and the men poured out. Few made it very far as guns were firing directly at them from above. When the battle ended, a handful of men remained alive. They stood under the cliffs out of range and sight of the enemy. They became the "beachhead" in enemy territory that the Allied commanders had hoped to establish. This assignment was accomplished at the cost of many lives. These men understood their mission and knew they were responsible to find a way to expand that beachhead. Their task was to take down the enemy guns overhead and secure a safe place where more Allied forces could arrive. As the film unfolded, their success in achieving their goal became a shared triumph for all who now know how critical the allied victory was.

Let us now focus on God's beachhead strategy. It started when He created the Garden and placed Adam there as resident steward. Following Adam, He worked with Abraham, Moses, Israel, and David to name a few. The ultimate beachhead was established through Christ, and has infiltrated the earth through His Body. Full occupation of earth hasn't taken place yet because some of the Church, especially the western section, has lost her military mindset. Others, like the Chinese Church, report for duty prepared to die, or to be tortured for the cause of the Kingdom.

Ever since the introduction of mankind to earth, God has purposed man to be the legal steward of this place. That God-given office of stewardship was established in the Garden and quickly became a hotly-contested prize, resulting in the earth being a war zone ever since. The coming of Christ to earth has shifted the battle line from a defensive one to an offensive one.

Every human being, born century after century, is a new recruit in the battle with the potential of serving in either army. It began with Adam and Eve. God told them to subdue the earth. Those instructions didn't refer to farming or herding. They were military commands. God knew their establishment on earth was being monitored, and that a power-maneuver would soon take place. When it did, Adam and Eve forgot their instructions, were taken captive, and the battle lines shifted.

The battle that engaged our original parents Adam and Eve, and now engages us, is not primarily a physical one, but is rather a battle of the mind and heart. The twisted weapon the enemy used against them wasn't about the act of eating. It was about their own thoughts and perceptions. The enemy's primary target was their perception of God and His Word. It was easy for the enemy to influence their choices once he succeeded in perverting their beliefs concerning God. It was also easy to separate them from God in their thoughts, and to turn them against one another, and later for their children Cain and Abel, to do the same.

Our mind is an interesting battlefield because God designed it with unique abilities intended to help us know and remember Him. These very abilities work against us when the source from which we receive information is not God. Consequently, instead of assimilating His truth, we absorb perverted facts like Adam and Eve did.

Our brains do not process information as facts, but as electrical impulses travelling through neurons. The brain interprets these impulses according to previously learned experiences. If these experiences are God-centered and therefore true, the resulting interpretation will be true. But if the previous experiences are distorted by influences such as lies or trauma, then the interpretation will be distorted and false.

Along with this intrinsic bent toward individualistic interpretation of life, our minds have other characteristics, which help or hinder us. A primary one is our western love of logic resulting in our aversion toward that which seems illogical or unreasonable. Another is the protective tendency of our minds. John and Paula Sanford of Elijah House Ministries teach that our brain is designed to be defensive, thus filtering and keeping out what seems unfamiliar or strange.

The Pharisees of Jesus' time were a perfect example of these principles in action. They were so steeped in tradition, religion and their own perception of God, that they could not hear or see Him in their midst. They were driven to hate and murder Him rather than to accept the living Truth. This brings us to the realization of how a leader's perception of God will influence many others.

Another battle line surfaces: our perceptions of God compared to His own perceptions of Himself. He has stated plainly that He does not perceive or process things the way we do, thus warning us that we must not rely on our minds to know Him:

> For My thoughts are not your thoughts, nor are your ways My ways, says the Lord. For as the heavens are higher than the earth, so are My ways higher than your ways and My thoughts than your thoughts (Isaiah 55:8,9 NKJV).

Even though He says it so clearly, we have difficulty believing it. When Satan told Adam and Eve they could be gods, and they bought into that lie, they lost the awe of God's words and came to think they could rely on their own thoughts and perceptions. We ourselves now carry this corruption in our DNA, and need God's help to grasp anything from Him that is spiritual, and especially anything unfamiliar to us.

I once learned an interesting lesson concerning perspective while doing a routine job of wallpapering. It was an interesting challenge due to the wallpaper's pattern and the structural variations in the small room. When I finished, I stood back and admired my work. Then the voice of my friend from the other doorway announced, "It's crooked!" As the shock passed, I moved next to her to see what could have gone wrong. It took me a few minutes of examining the walls from various angles and from certain points in the room to discover that the symmetry of the wallpaper appeared to change according to the angle at which one stood. It actually seemed to move when I changed position. From either side it looked uneven, but when viewed from a central point, it was perfect.

My wallpaper analogy is a simple example of how our perception, hearing and understanding can be easily distorted, based on our limited perspective of circumstances.

The issue of perspective and perception is one of the greatest challenges in our personal lives, relationships and corporateness. What do we mean by the term perspective? The *American Heritage Dictionary* says this:

Per•spec•tive (p...r-spμk"t¹v) n. .
1. The technique of representing three-dimensional objects and depth relationships on a two-dimensional surface.
2. a. view or vista,
   b. A mental view or outlook: "It is useful occasionally to look at the past to gain a perspective on the present" (Fabian Linden).
3. The appearance of objects in depth as perceived by normal binocular vision.
4. The relationship of aspects of a subject to each other and to a whole: a perspective of history;
5. a. need to view the problem in the proper perspective.
   b. Subjective evaluation of relative significance; a point of view: the perspective of the displaced homemaker.
   c. The ability to perceive things in their actual interrelations or comparative importance: tried to keep my perspective throughout the crisis.

per•spec•tive adj. Of, relating to, seen, or represented in perspective.[1]

Dealing with perspective needs some caution and consideration. It concerns:

a) what one is looking at, or hearing or feeling,
b) one's position while looking, hearing or feeling, and
c) what one already believes in relation to what one is looking at, hearing, feeling or learning.

Our Redeemer-Husband: Our Head

What a powerful mixture of the subjective and the objective! It reminds me of taking flight lessons – especially of being trained to land a small private plane on a runway. I learned that it is very important to start the approach for landing with accurate and keen judgment of wind, speed, and distance. Then it is critical to re-check these perceptions at various junctions, making whatever adjustments are necessary to ensure that the plane lands properly on the earth – a very good idea!

Similarly, what we think or believe about something, and how we respond to it, determines the outcome. With flying, especially a small plane, every distortion of perception and judgment can create major problems with destination and landing. If you have never been at the controls of a plane, try thinking of golfing, or any other highly coordinated activity that relies heavily on perceptions. The point is that our perspectives and perceptions govern our judgment and decisions, and therefore our lives.

Our ability to perceive is affected by many variables, most of which are familiar. God has given us five natural senses, along with spiritual ones, through which to receive and evaluate life's data. Our upbringing and education form these perceptions into set patterns for life. As an example, a family raised and educated in New York City will perceive life differently than one living in rural Saskatchewan.

Our church affiliations influence cultural perspectives as well. The various branches of Christianity have certain set views that are taught over and above the foundational basics of the Bible. For example, one of the classic differences in point of view has to do with eschatology (the study of the end times). Some groups debate and argue about the teachings of pre-trib(ulation), mid-trib, post-trib, and a-trib. These differences are very well known. One could add issues of baptism, ministry methods, church priorities, dress codes, and social issues, to name a few. My first church family taught, among other things, that Sunday newspapers and movies (at the theater) were things to avoid in the Christian life. A few years later I relocated and my next church family said those areas were not significant issues. They emphasized the "more critical" matters of abstinence from alcohol and giving to the poor. These are just a few simple examples of the way variations in church tradition can influence one group compared to another.

My topic, headship, is another subject that can be viewed from various angles, in different church groups. It can encompass everything from, *I'm head of myself*, to some human being having absolute authority over another. Since this is the main subject, we need to define *Head*.

The Greek word for Head is *kephale*. Both Vine's [2a] and Holman's [2b] dictionaries give extensive critiques of this word. The full definitions are in the Appendix. Here is a summary.

a) uppermost part of the body
b) first, top, chief
c) a pre-eminent relationship
d) Christ as foundation of a spiritual building
e) summit of a mountain
f) representing a whole person
g) a beginning or source
h) the foremost person
i) a leader \ chief \ prince
j) the first in a series

This list presents many perspectives of headship, and we will wrestle together with some of these ideas so that we can find a deeper place in God's heart concerning His meaning, when He speaks of headship.

We must ask ourselves some questions. The key issue is: Are we aligned with the Captain of the Host, the Head of the Church, and are we therefore completely under His loving government? Or are we limited to the natural world, our own inadequate resources and our own attempts to overcome? Do we have His perspective or only our own, which is so highly affected by ungodly influences? These questions represent various perspectives and points of view that contribute to our struggle to understand each other, our circumstances and God.

Often we are deeply into "survival" rather than looking into establishing or expanding a beachhead. Frequently we are more consumed with our appearance and the behavior of others, rather than with a strategic analysis of the battle raging around us and the urgency to discern our part in it.

The ultimate battle and establishment of the most important beachhead was the coming of Christ to earth. Like at Omaha Beach, Jesus established a "beachhead" on earth with much opposition. The story of His life is filled with major contentions: from the flight out of Bethlehem to the attacks of the Pharisees accusing Him of blasphemy because He claimed to be one with God the Father. They tried stoning Him, ridiculing Him and running Him out of town. I'm sure the disciples held their breath many times and were surprised because the angry Jews were so unsuccessful in their attempts to harm Jesus.

Even though the battle seemed to culminate with Jesus' crucifixion on the Cross, in some ways it really had only just begun. There were still many expansion challenges and battles to come. After Jesus was resurrected He appeared to His disciples and exhorted and commissioned them: "...as the Father has sent me, I also send you" (John 20:21). Then He told them:

> Thus it is written and thus it was necessary for
> the Christ to suffer and to rise from the dead on
> the third day, and that repentance and remission of sins should be preached in His name
> to all nations beginning at Jerusalem. And you

are witnesses of these things. Behold I send the Promise of My Father upon you; but tarry in the city of Jerusalem until you are endued with power from on high (Luke 24:46-49 NKJV).

He was preparing them for battle. This battle continued throughout New Testament times and still rages today. Some of the current issues of contention are:

a) Who is the real God? Is the Moslem, or Mormon "God" the same as the Judeo-Christian One?
b) Who is the real Christ as opposed to a religious version of Him?
c) What is His true and rightful authority?
d) Who is really head over my life, and/or the Church?
e) Is the Church victorious over evil in all aspects?
f) How do we define the real Church?

Next, we will explore what the Word says about headship and how it works in living reality.

Endnotes

1. American Heritage Talking Dictionary., Softkey International Inc. Cambridge, MA.USA
2. [a]Vine's Complete Expository Dictionary, W.E.Vine, Merrill F. Unger, William White Jr., Thomas Nelson Inc., Nashville, Tenn. 1984
   [b] Holman Bible Dictionary, Quick Verse Bible Software

Chapter 3
THREE LEVELS OF HEADSHIP

Headship is one dimension of the multi-faceted wonder of the relationship within the Godhead: Father, Son and Spirit. God has extended a dimension of Himself through Christ becoming Head of the Church. The foundation of headship is His love, and through its development on various levels, He releases a larger measure of this love to us as Christ's Body. Headship creates divine connectedness, resulting in a oneness, beyond anything that humans can do themselves. This connectedness releases the flow of divine life.

The Father, Son and Spirit experience a higher order of oneness among themselves than is possible for God to share with His people. In the book *The Shack*, Papa explains the relationship this way:

> "To begin with, that you can't grasp the wonder of my nature is rather a good thing. Who wants to worship a God who can be fully comprehended, eh? Not much mystery in that."
>
> (Mack asks) "But what difference does it make that there are three of you, and you are all one God? Did I say that right?"

(Papa answers) "Right enough".... "It makes all the difference in the world!".... "We are not three gods, and we are not talking about one god with three attitudes, like a man who is a husband, father, and worker. I am one God and I am three persons and each of the three is fully and entirely the one"....

"...What's important is this: If I were simply one God and only one Person, then you would find yourself in this creation without something wonderful, without something essential even. And I would be utterly other than I am."

(Mack asks) "And we would be without...?"

(Papa goes on) "Love and relationship. All love and relationship is possible for you only because it already exists within Me, within God myself. Love is not the limitation; Love is the flying. I am Love.

"...You do understand...that unless I had an object to love – or more accurately a someone to love – if I did not have such a relationship within myself, then I would not be capable of love at all?"[1]

God has made His love and life the central point of all, and that's what headship reflects. He wants us to share in the oneness of Himself; to be able to enter into His divine corporateness. When man refused to continue in the simplicity of oneness in the Garden, God brought forth the deeper connection to Himself through re-birth and headship. It's all about relationship, not structure, as some believe. And even so, it's not just about any relationship. It's about God's relationship with those who have been born anew of divine Spirit and Blood, by Christ and are part of His divine connection between Heaven and earth.

God desired to display and impart His divine love for us through His Son. We needed our hearts to be touched by the manifestation of God's love in His Son to prepare us to believe and accept Christ's work of redemption. God wanted us to be in relational oneness with the Son, as many sons, so He could impart the fullness of the Godhead to us. Christ is the gateway, or door as He calls Himself, for us to return to oneness with our God. Andrew Murray expresses this wonderfully in his book, *The Holiest of All*:

> Because, as the Son, it is He alone in whom the unapproachable and utterly incomprehensible glory of God is made manifest, through whom as Mediator the uncreated God, and the works of His hand, can come into contact and fellowship.
>
> His relation to creation rests on His relation to the Father. He is the out-shining of God's glory, and the express image of His substance. As we only know the sun by the light that shines from it, so is Christ, the outshining, the revelation of God's glory. As the light that shines from the sun is of the same nature with it, so the Son is of one nature with the Father – God of God. And as a son bears the likeness of his father, because he has his life and nature from him, so the Son of God is the express image of His substance. He is of one substance with the Father– His express image – and hath therefore life in Himself, even as the Father hath life in Himself. [2] (underlining mine).

The Godhead's redemptive plan with the coming of the glorious Son to earth revealed the love and wonder of God and His heavenly realm to His people in a fuller measure than anyone could ever have experienced or imagined. Even now, little do we really comprehend the wonder and glory of God coming forth in this way, or the power of headship when it is manifest through Him.

God purposed headship to be displayed on three levels, as Paul expresses:

> But I want you to understand that <u>Christ is the head</u> of every man, and the <u>husband is the head</u> of his wife, and <u>God is the head</u> of Christ (1 Corinthians 11:3, NRSV, underlining mine).

This verse reveals the complete design of godly headship with its three key levels; it is from one of Paul's letters that deals with order in the Church, particularly the proper way for men and women to pray or prophesy in public. The context addresses broad Christian principles and cultural standards of that time. Paul emphatically states he wants us to understand this issue.

Since the title "Christ" (the Messiah; the Anointed One), is used so centrally in this verse, we understand that this statement on headship deals primarily with God's redemptive plan for the earth: thus the mention of Christ's headship of man being first in the set of three. For our study we will begin with the highest level: "God is the head of Christ".

Level 1: Father and Son

The Father and Holy Spirit, along with the angels, assisted the Son in His trip to earth. As He arrived, Jesus came with a divine seal – His Father's headship. This was a key element of the new dimension of their relationship: a heavenly Father with an earthly Son. It was important for the earthly Son to have His Father's Kingdom with Him: a portable Heaven. This compares to an embassy in a foreign country and Jesus was the ambassador. The headship was His seal of office, and His presence was the new beachhead here.

Each member of the Godhead had a primary role to play in

this battle strategy. Father God manifested divine Fatherliness (i.e. love, authority, provision) from Heaven to earth toward Jesus, while Jesus manifested Sonship (i.e. love, devotion, obedience) back toward the Father from earth to Heaven. They would "dance" a Father-Son "dance" together creating a link relationally between the Kingdom in Heaven and the Kingdom on earth. Holy Spirit would come upon Jesus at His baptism, and work with Him while He completed His earthly mission, and then would be poised "in the wings" to make His grand appearance to man at Pentecost.

The two main ingredients for headship are God's love and God's authority which He manifests out of His multi-faceted being. Let us examine each of these:

God's love: Headship is therefore rooted in, and dependent upon, love expressed through a covenantal relationship either between the Father and Son, Christ and His Church, or husband and wife. Headship can only function the way God intended, if it is founded on a loving, relationally-based covenant. Oneness of Head and Body becomes a living reality through the love on which the covenant rests. Headship is not a matter of obedience to the law, or of submission to a man-made structure of authority. When headship operates the way God intended, two hearts are connected, functioning as one.

God's authority: Headship is grounded in God's throne of power and government; every level of Kingdom authority must be connected to Him to be legitimate, as with an ambassador who must be connected to a genuine government. All other forms of authority, not grounded in God's authority, are false.

These are the primary ways God relates His Kingdom to earth and to its inhabitants. His purpose is two-fold: the revelation of Himself in His fullness, and the fulfillment of His plan for all mankind and for the earth.

Level 2: Christ and His Church

When Christ Jesus completed His earthly assignment on the Cross He emerged as the glorified Son of Man and Son of God. The power and light released when He was on the Cross was like an atomic blast that shook the earth so violently that the dead were ejected from their graves. God tore apart the curtain that separated the Holy of Holies, keeping His *Shekinah* glory confined, and separate from His people. He no longer would abide in a physical building such as that temple. He no longer required animal sacrifices or religious rituals. He was birthing a new race of humans: redeemed sons through the Blood of Christ.

Redemption is a powerful event and only true redemption could birth the new Body / Church. Christ was "redeemed" from the grave, and came forth in resurrection life. His disciples, along with everyone redeemed since, received Holy Spirit and were born again into Christ's life: resurrection Life. We too are bought and paid for; every aspect of our being is now owned by Him. We are redeemed (bought back) not only from the curse of death resulting from sin, but also from the very root of sin and iniquity. We are redeemed back to a point before sin, and to our origin in God. As the redeemed ones in Him, we are His living Body functioning on earth.

He stood as the Head of this new Body being formed. His disciples were grafted to the Head by Holy Spirit who had entered them. Holy Spirit became the "power cord," like our spinal cord, that links the head and body causing it to function as one unit.

Christ purchased this Body through a covenant with Father God and Holy Spirit. It was forged in His own Blood. He promised His followers the Pentecost visitation and He delivered. Those born of Spirit were now connected to Him as one, and the resulting flow of divine life was obvious. His Body was alive and working well on earth.

Level 3: Husband and wife

Marriage, God's way, is also about a covenantal relationship
– a forging of two into one. This covenant should be initiated
by God Himself and activated by the man and woman who
are joining together in marriage. A marriage covenant in and
with God, is more powerful than the legal ceremony that the
government or that religion offers. In order for godly headship
to operate within a Christian couple's marriage, they need to
be in covenant with God and with each other. This creates the
"power cord" that connects God and His Kingdom to their
relationship and home.

A few years ago friends shared with me their discovery
concerning headship in their home. They had been troubled
by the lack of unity in their marriage and had struggled to
find a resolution to the conflict. Each tried advising the other
on how to change, while they were ardently seeking God's
wisdom. Then one day the light of God's truth entered their
hearts. They realized that though they were married as Christians, they had not, due to ignorance, made a covenant with
each other at the time of their marriage.

As they gained insight into the meaning of a covenant, they
came to the conclusion that without a true covenant they were
not fully connected. They decided to re-commit themselves in
a new marriage ceremony during a 25th wedding anniversary
celebration, that included the establishment of a covenant with
God and each other. They were delightfully amazed at the
change in their hearts and the resulting harmony that began
to manifest in their lives.

Headship must become a mutual commitment that is empowered through love and respect within a true covenantal
relationship, and cannot work without it. This is especially

true in marriage, but also in a local church. Love, within the bond of that covenant prevents headship from deteriorating into harshness, imposed authority, or a vacuum, thus negating true headship.

The power within a loving covenantal relationship, either in a church or in a marriage, is God's weapon of choice for re-taking the earth. Each manifestation of that divine covenant becomes a functioning extension of His beachhead.

The levels of this new portable government structure called headship can be compared with one another based on similarities and differences thus helping us to understand more of God's intention for headship. It will also allow us to explore further the substitution of human headship in the Church for the headship of Christ.

Endnotes

1. *The Shack.* William Young. Windblown Media, Los Angeles, California. 2007, Pages 101,102.
2. *The Holiest of All.* Andrew Murray. Whitaker House, 30 Hunt Valley Circle, New Kensington, PA. 15068. 1996, Page 40.

Chapter 4

CHRIST'S OWN HEAD

When Christ the Messiah emerged from the heavenly realm and stepped into the arena of humanity, He continued in a different way to have full relationship of oneness with the Godhead. He came forth as God's firstborn Son on earth. The Godhead, who together as Elohim (Father, Son and Holy Spirit), are, were, and always will be one in totality and essence. God is not divided with this change, but expanded through a new creative maneuver.

As He the promised One, emerges on earth with headship established for Him, the Kingdom of God (God's family business) enters a new stage of execution. Godly love and government are established on earth in and through this unique person. It seems most appropriate to examine the origin of headship in order to gain a foundation from which to understand the other levels that have developed from, and depend upon it. Our previous verse states, "and God is the head of Christ" (1Corinthians 11:3, NRSV).

The Messiah had been prophesied and promised for many centuries, as recorded first in Genesis 3:15. God spoke and Christ came as the Son – breaking forth with light at a new daybreak – and entered history. God the Son has always existed, as we are told in John 1:1- 5:

> In the beginning was the Word, and the Word was with God, and the Word was God. He was in the beginning with God. All things were made through Him, and without Him nothing was made that was made. In Him was life, and the life was the light of men. And the light shines in the darkness, and the darkness did not comprehend it (NKJV).

We barely understand what this means!

Throughout the Old Testament we catch glimpses of Him that become clearer on this side of the Cross (A.D.). The various aspects or facets of God became more evident with the advent of Christ and subsequently, Holy Spirit. Thus we see the struggle of the Pharisees and Sadducees: they could not comprehend that their God would change His form, especially to that of a human.

When Christ came to earth as the Sacrificial Lamb for you and me, He did not appear in His divine glory. The Word says He laid down all He was, and all He had:

> Let the same mind be in you that was in Christ Jesus, who, though he was in the form of God, did not regard equality with God as something to be exploited, but <u>emptied Himself, taking the form of a slave, being born in human likeness. And being found in human form, He humbled Himself</u> and became obedient to the point of death-- even death on a cross (Philippians. 2: 5-8, NRSV, underlining mine).

The emptying and humbling mentioned in this passage concerns the preparatory positioning of the Son for His work here on earth and beyond. His death began when He emptied Himself. How do we comprehend what He did? Kelly Varner describes it this way:

> He who was rich became poor. The Word was made flesh. He condescended from the realm of perfect order and worship to the lower realm of death and chaos. He identified with broken humanity, and, as such, lowered Himself into a relationship of authority and submission to the Father. Prior to that He and the Father were one. He lowered Himself even further and submitted to Joseph and Mary.[1]

God – Father, Son and Holy Spirit – orchestrated a plan to establish mankind on earth as His stewards who would manifest the Kingdom of God on the earth. When mankind failed, God was ready to thwart the stronghold of Satan that had entered the heart of mankind and therefore the earth.

Pride was, and is Satan's downfall, and with it he poisoned Adam and Eve. The antidote to pride is humility. Humility is the very core of God's nature and therefore of Heaven. In his book *Humility*, Andrew Murray says "...and so Jesus came to bring humility back to earth, to make us partakers of it, and by it to save us."[2] As God's creatures, our response must be to humble ourselves before Him. Murray continues:

> ....the first and chief mark of the relation of the creature, the secret of His blessedness, is the humility and nothingness which leave God free to be all[3] (underlining mine).

Christ embodied this "humility and nothingness" by emptying Himself in submission to His Father, and gladly aligning Himself under His Father's headship. Headship is the hallmark of God's Kingdom on earth. Adam had lived under a type of headship in the Garden, but he lost it when he chose another's will over God's. Christ Jesus brought it back with His inception.

Murray defines humility as the place of entire dependence on God. Thus there is no other plan or source of life for the family of God. Jesus understood that, and lived dependent on His Father all His life. His words and actions were permeated with the fragrance of humility. He understood Kingdom order and that being under His Father's headship would position Him to receive everything He needed to succeed in His journey on earth.

Our triune God had a plan from the beginning:

> And I will put enmity
> Between you and the woman,
> And between your seed and her Seed;
> He shall bruise your head,
> And you shall bruise His heel (Genesis 3:15 NKJV).

The emergence of Christ and the development of His headship engaged both love and war. Satan appeared to have won the round in the Garden, but God had a plan that would remove his usurped authority and use him to further His own plans. God had an invasion plan that He first processed through a man (Abraham). He then extended the plan to include a family (Jews in Israel) which made possible the final stage of invasion, the coming of a Son (Jesus). But each of these partners in the war plan was potentially fallible.

Finally the stage was set for the promised One, but could Christ succeed perfectly? His assignment was the most critical maneuver, and He had limited Himself. There were rules for this war. Only a man in a proper submitted relationship with

44

God, could win back the authority that Adam lost. Authority had been given to a man, and only another human could redeem it.

The first Adam lost his God-given position of authority over the earth through doubt and disobedience which opened him to the poison of pride. Immediately he became self-conscious and defensive and hid himself from God. The Son/Adam won back that lost authority: He accomplished it through love and humble submission with obedience. This is why it was imperative for Him to lay down all His glory and majesty. He could not operate as God in His assignment since He had to function as a man, using the weapon available to all of us, our God-given gift of freedom of choice, to love and obey our heavenly Father. In the same way our submission to God's authority connects us to His supernatural presence and His warring arsenal, which includes mighty angels.

Just as Adam (the name refers to both man and woman while they were in the Garden) lived in God's presence before the Fall, so Christ lived on earth in the divine presence in a similar atmosphere called headship. A picture comes to mind of Jesus walking on earth under God's covenant-rainbow with the Father's love and His governmental rule as an umbrella over His head. Jesus lived under an open Heaven, or an extension of Heaven, through which He operated while He was here with us. The supernatural life that Christ now shares with us, who live in Him, is a heavenly beachhead in enemy territory and a brilliant spot of light in this world of sin and darkness. John states:

> In Him was life, and that life was the light of men. The light shines in the darkness, but the darkness has not understood it (John 1:4,5, NIV, underlining mine).

45

Paul's scriptural metaphor in 1 Corinthians 12:4-27, uses the imagery of the human body to describe the parallel way Christ's Body functions in its diversity. It gives us a better understanding of body-life with a head and body working together. This metaphor also provides a deeper understanding of the other levels of headship and establishes that the head and the body function together as one unit. On this foundational level Father God in Heaven is the Head, and Christ the Son on earth is His Body. God's Body becomes visible, touchable and audible.

Jesus said in John 14:9 (NIV), "Anyone who has seen me has seen the Father." He meant it literally. The human Jesus was the embodiment of the Father, as He says in John 10:38, (NIV) "The Father is in me and I in the Father," thus His title, Emmanuel – God with us. The very essence of God's life is being manifest in human form, indwelt with Holy Spirit.

To further examine this embodiment I have chosen to use three primary elements related to the definition of headship:

a) authority
b) submission
c) oneness.

I believe these three elements can be found on all three levels of the headship structure mentioned in 1 Corinthians 11, and will give us a tool for exploring and comparing them. Here is how they manifest on the first level with God and Christ.

Authority

1) **Father God** as the Head is the source of *all* authority which He manifests through His love. As previously stated, any authority outside His Kingdom is illegitimate. God has ways of revealing His rightful authority in every circumstance, like

in His appearance to Moses at the burning bush. His presence has a way of settling the issue. His will must be accomplished and His Word must be fulfilled. There is no other choice. When He said, "Let there be light," there was no other option but for light to appear. His ability to bring forth the Christ was another demonstration of His authority.

2) **The Son** made it very clear that He was on earth under His Father's authority. Jesus indicated this many times: "I can do nothing on my own. As I hear, I judge; and my judgment is just, because I seek to do not my own will but the will of him who sent me" (John 5:30, NRSV). He was aligned as one in will and purpose with His Father. He refused independence. He chose for the Father to be seen and heard through Him, and humbled Himself so that the Father could be all!

The issue of His authority on earth is often discussed in Scripture because it was constantly challenged by the Jewish leaders. The Roman Centurion (see Matthew 8) saw what the Jewish leaders had missed. He recognized the principle of authority in action (someone under authority has authority themselves and what they decree is manifested) because he had experienced it in the Roman military and saw that it was demonstrated in Jesus' life. He knew that with a command from Jesus the deed would be done.

The life Jesus lived as a model for us demonstrated the Father's love, authority and power flowing through a person truly submitted. We gaze in awe as nature and the powers of darkness yielded to His commands. Winds and storms ceased, food multiplied, disease and even death fled, demons begged for mercy, and, anger, hatred and prejudice were overcome. People were amazed at Jesus' teachings, the kindness He showed and the authority He demonstrated. They had never seen anyone express God's love and authority as He did. Neither had anyone expressed knowledge of Father God like He did, speaking even of personal relationship with Him. No one had ever lived as a Kingdom citizen fully understanding almighty God's love, government and authority, as He did.

Submission

Jesus submitted to His Father, His Head, completely and gladly. He said "Very truly, I tell you, the Son can do nothing on His own, but only what He sees the Father doing; for whatever the Father does, the Son does likewise" (John 5:19, NRSV). Their corporate life affected everything He did.

Jesus was bound by love to the plan of the Godhead; He was not on a personal crusade. He, with His Father and Holy Spirit were functioning together as *one*: Father as the Head, Jesus as the Body, and Holy Spirit providing the supernatural Life-flow for the mission. They were one in heart and purpose. The Body had *no existence* without the Head; the Head had *no presence* without the Body; they flowed together as one, with Holy Spirit synergizing it to work.

Christ knew that submission and humility were not a shame or a hindrance as pride would have one believe, but instead they brought Heaven to earth for Him and His purpose. He knew that the only way for Him to gain His inheritance as a Son, was to be in loving oneness with and in submission to His Father. Similarly, the only way for us to become sons of God and to share in the inheritance, is through our joining as one with Jesus in His Sonship, as the only true Son.

Oneness

In the corporate oneness and loving unity of Father, Son and Holy Spirit, are found all beauty and symmetry. It is a symphony of glory and wonder too awesome to describe with human language; it can only be experienced by one's spirit, in tune with His Spirit, and made possible through His Blood.

When flying over the Grand Canyon, I profoundly experienced natural beauty but to a far lesser degree. The panorama of majesty and beauty rendered me speechless. Words seemed like a smudge. The intensity of attempting to describe the oneness between Father and Son is far more overwhelming. The light and love are blinding in their purity and strength. It is far easier to describe what their oneness does.

Within this oneness is found all life and provision. The Son knew that all the Father had was His: no hesitation, no short supply, no need or want unmet. We get a glimpse of the incredible love between them as this earthly drama unfolds: the Father moving Heaven and earth, to bring forth Jesus and to care for Him in every way; the Son pouring His life back to the Father in all love, submission and honor, even unto death. They each know their part and fulfill it perfectly.

Here is headship in living Technicolor: perfection! This magnificent oneness brought the wonder and glory of God's supernatural life to earth through the Son. The miraculous interaction between Jesus and all that was around Him caused it to be observable: when He taught and when He touched people (the sick, the crippled, the dead, and the blind); when He rebuked storms or devils; when He prayed over the food and it multiplied.

His presence alone changed people like Zacchaeus (see Luke 19:2), who responded to the touch of Holy Spirit emanating through Jesus. The power of Holy Spirit overcame what had previously bound him and manifested the Scripture "Not by might nor by power, but by My Spirit, says the Lord of hosts" (Zechariah. 4:6 b NKJV).

This is our model for living the Spirit-filled life in Christ. Jesus came to overcome through love and humble submission and to offer us this overcoming power through His divine presence resident in each one connected to Him. His victory over sin and death on the Cross, His resurrection and our redemption together make it possible for His supernatural life to indwell us by His Spirit. This is overcoming!

Headship between the Father and the Son with all its glory and power forms the pattern we need for examining the next two levels effectively.

Endnotes

1. *The Priesthood is Changing.* Kelly Varner. Destiny Image Publishers Inc., PO Box 351, Shippensburg, PA., 17257-0315. 1991. Page 73.
2. *Humility.* Andrew Murray. Bridge –Logos, Gainsville, Florida, 32614. 2000, Page 2,3.
3. *Ibid. Page 4*

Chapter 5

CHRIST'S POSITION AS HEAD

From His birth, Jesus lived in relationship with His heavenly Father as His head, and then He became Head of the Church at her birthing. When the resurrected Christ completed His earthly appointment and entered Heaven as the great High Priest and victorious Son seated at the right hand of the Majesty on high, a whole new dynamic unfolded on earth, with a further level of headship being established.

While He was on earth His disciples experienced the covering and connection of His headship with His Father. As they submitted to His authority, they shared in it, and experienced the divine supernatural Life-flow through Holy Spirit. They had authority to speak in His name, and His Kingdom was manifest. As we read the Gospels we find that the disciples were surprised and amazed when that happened.

At His departure (ascension), He said it was better that He should go (see John 16) and He promised another would come. He told them to wait for this promised One, and as they obeyed, it was fulfilled during the Feast of Pentecost. When Holy Spirit came like "a wind and tongues of fire" (Acts 2) they were electrified with divine heavenly power and the Church

(Ekklesia – legislative assembly) became a living organism, Head and Body made one, infused with God's supernatural life – the *real* Big Bang!

With this new birthing a fresh dimension of headship came into being. The Son already had total authority over mankind as God: "But I want you to understand that Christ is the Head of every man," (1Corinthians 11:3, NRSV). Another divine headship is now manifest with God's newborn Kingdom sons – His business partners.

To further understand the depth of His headship, let us examine these references:

> In Him we have redemption through His blood, the forgiveness of sins, in accordance with the riches of God's grace that He lavished on us with all wisdom and understanding. And He made known to us the mystery of His will according to His good pleasure, which He purposed in Christ, to be put into effect when the times will have reached their fulfillment—to bring all things in Heaven and on earth together under one Head, even Christ" (Ephesians 1: 7-10, NIV, underlining mine.)

> ...which He worked in Christ when He raised Him from the dead and seated Him at His right hand in the heavenly places, far above all principality and power and might and dominion, and every name that is named, not only in this age but also in that which is to come. And He put all things under His feet, and gave Him to be head over all things to the church" (Ephesians 1:20-22, NKJV, underlining mine).

But speaking the truth in love, we must grow up in every way <u>into Him who is the Head, into Christ</u>, from whom the whole Body, joined and knit together by every ligament with which it is equipped, as each part is working properly, promotes the Body's growth in building itself up in love (Ephesians 4:15-16, NRSV, underlining mine).

These three references primarily state that:

- Everything in Heaven and on earth will be brought together under Christ's headship in the fulfillment of time.
- Christ is the head of every "man" ("anything of human origin" according to *Vine's Complete Expository Dictionary*).
- Christ has all rule and authority over every dominion, power, and name.
- Christ is Head of His Church Body.

The vastness of Christ's authority and headship is evident. All natural authority pales in comparison. Christ's headship over His Body, the Church, is our focus. Here is how *Holman's Bible Dictionary* defines headship:

Head of the Church: A title for Christ (Eph. 4:15; Col. 1:18). In Ephesians, the metaphor of Christ as head of His body, the church, is carefully developed.

Headship includes the idea of Christ's authority (1:22; 5:23) and of the submission required of the church (5:24). More is in view than a statement of Christ's authority. The focus is on the character of Christ's relationship with the church. Unlike self-seeking human lords (Luke 22:25), Christ exercises His authority for the church (Eph. 1:22 NRSV, NIV), nourishing and caring for the church as one cares for one's own body (5:29). Christ's headship also points to the interrelationship of Christ and the church. The mystery of husband and wife becoming "one flesh" is applied to Christ and the church (5:31), which is "the fullness of him that filleth all in all" (1:23). In Colossians 1:18, the idea of Christ as head is again complex, including not only the idea of head as authority but of head as source (1:15-20). The church is called to follow its head and to rest secure in its relationship with Him.[1]

This headship of Christ is also relationally based, and that releases all His love and authority into the life of His Body. The magnitude of His authority is expressed through His titles: King of Kings and Lord of Lords.

In order for His headship to become the connection of a living head and body, the life of God had to enter man. It began at Pentecost: humankind was transfused with divine Life, and transformed by Holy Spirit. This was the living seed promised by God to Abraham: "The promises were spoken to Abraham and to his seed. The Scripture does not say 'and to seeds,' meaning many people, but 'and to your seed,' meaning one person, who is Christ" (Galatians 3:16, NIV). Scripture tells us He is the author of life and everything is sustained by Him.

That supernatural life manifesting on earth began when Abraham's and Sarah's "dead" bodies were touched by God to bring forth the promised son Isaac. Later the divine seed entered Mary and a virgin conceived the "Son of God, Son of man" child who became the one seed planted in order to bring forth many seeds. Now that supernatural seed of the Spirit of Christ is implanted into every heart that receives Him by faith. Just as our physical seed carries our DNA from generation to generation, the seed of the Spirit of Christ carries God's DNA into our being, to manifest His life within. The Church is a living organism, a Body, comprised of many Blood-bought cells (sons) each functioning with God's life.

On Level 1, the headship-relationship of Father and Son is connected in essence (Head–Body) to Himself because He and Christ are one. All was perfect in that match and process. There was no iniquity, rebellion or sin to interfere. But when God wants to work with a man on earth, new challenges come into play; "I looked for a man among them who would build up the wall and stand before me in the gap on behalf of the land so I would not have to destroy it, but I found none" (Ezekiel 22:30, NIV). God needed to make a new divine connection with man in order to fully function with him.

On Level 2, we have God/Christ as Head partnering with redeemed man as His Body. Only the power of the Cross and the Blood could make it possible for this holy, almighty God to literally enter into, and join Himself in covenant, with redeemed man.

Conversion is necessary to enable us, sinful humans, to partner in covenant with God. *Funk & Wagnall's Dictionary* defines "conversion" thus: "The act of converting, or the state of being converted."

Then it defines <u>convert</u>:

- To change into another state, form or substance; transform.
- To apply or adapt to a new or different purpose or use. [2]

Conversion is a drastic process requiring true change, or metamorphosis. Redemption is not just a little adjustment, but a powerful exchange of life. Our old life was "purchased" and exchanged for a new, corporate life in Christ. We no longer own our old lives which are "crucified with Christ," but now have entered a new existence. We are 'seated with Christ in heavenly places'. (Ephesians 2:6)

There are too many "non-converted" people in the Church, primarily because we leaders have not taught, or modeled true "death of the old man" (conversion), which in turn leaves them puzzled and guilty as to why their lives have not changed. We have blurred the clear line Jesus made between the issues of life and death. He didn't go to the Cross because we needed a little fixing, but because we needed to die, and He did it for us so we could die in Him and then live in Him. He has redeemed us from the false gods of evil and self.

Too many people are mental believers only and not true disciples (corporate ones). They have head knowledge of the doctrines and principles of Christianity without having experienced a real death of the old self, which can only be accomplished by faith in the finished work of Christ on His Cross, and a true entrance into the divine life of Christ. That faith gives access to His supernatural, resurrection life. Andrew Murray says it this way:

> The Holy Spirit could come down as the spirit of the God-man – actually the Spirit of God, and yet as truly the spirit of man. He could come down as the Spirit of the glorified Jesus, to be in each one who believes in Jesus, the Spirit of His personal life, and His personal presence, and at the same time the spirit of the personal life of the believer. Just as in Jesus the perfect union of God and man had been affected and finally completed when He sat down on the throne and He so entered on a new stage of existence, a glory hitherto unknown; now also, a new era has commenced in the life of and the work of the Spirit. He can now come down to witness of the perfect union of the divine and

the human. In becoming our life, He makes us partakers of it. There is now the Spirit of the glorified Jesus: He has poured Him forth; we have received Him to stream into us, through us, and forth from us in rivers of blessing.[3]

When individuals choose by faith to enter into the covenant Christ made by His Blood (to be "born again"), they enter a transformation, a metamorphosis, a dramatic life change. They are no longer just their "old selves." They are now in partnership – Head/Body relationship – with Christ through Holy Spirit. A whole new life form comes into existence – man re-joined with God, because he has been redeemed. "Abide in Me and I in you" (John 15:4). All of man's limitations and inabilities are now *owned* by Christ, and we *own* all His limitlessness and power manifest through the glorified Spirit of Christ within. What a deal! Wonder of wonders!

In the same way that Jesus needed headship under which to function here on earth as God's Body, so the Church – Jesus' Body – needs headship in order to fully function. God's love and governmental rule is the Church's heavenly umbrella. It provides heavenly blessing and covering for her life and growth along with the power to function as an overcomer and conqueror. It is an extension of the heavenly beachhead.

The Church, like Christ on the first level, has to respond and be fully connected in love to her Head. The degree of heavenly life and coverage depends on how connected the Church is to His love and authority in headship, her degree of submission, and their oneness. Let's examine these aspects again in Christ's headship-relationship with the Church.

Authority

1. The authority of this new Head, Christ, is abso-

lute. His position of supremacy has no question or limit. The Apostle John experienced His love, glory and authority while on the Isle of Patmos, and spoke of it in the Book of Revelation:

> Then I turned to see whose voice it was that spoke to me, and on turning I saw seven golden lampstands, and in the midst of the lampstands I saw one like the Son of Man, clothed with a long robe and with a golden sash across his chest. His head and His hair were white as white wool, white as snow; His eyes were like a flame of fire, His feet were like burnished bronze, refined as in a furnace, and His voice was like the sound of many waters. In His right hand He held seven stars, and from His mouth came a sharp, two-edged sword, and His face was like the sun shining with full force (Revelation 1:12-16, NRSV).

He is the majestic One! His name is above all names (see Philippians 2:9); all judgment has been placed in His hands, (see Acts 10:42); He is called the Chief Shepherd, (see 1 Peter 5:4); the Bridegroom (see John 3:29); He is the Commander-in-Chief, and His supremacy is perfect:

> He is the image of the invisible God, the first-born over all creation. For by Him all things were created that are in Heaven and that are on earth, visible and invisible, whether thrones or dominions or principalities or powers. All things were created through Him and for Him. And He is before all things, and in Him all things consist. And He is the head of the Body, the Church, who is the beginning, the firstborn

from the dead, that in all things He may have
the preeminence. For it pleased the Father that
in Him all the fullness should dwell, and by
Him to reconcile all things to Himself, by Him,
whether things on earth or things in Heaven,
having made peace through the blood of His
cross (Colossians 1:15-20, NKJV).

This is the Church's divine Head! Wow! What more could we
hope or ask for?

2. Now let's discuss the new Body, the Church (Ekklesia)
that is united with Christ. The Church is both under His authority (headship) and functions through His authority just as
He walked on earth functioning as His Father's Body. As the
Church is fully connected (with all submission and love), to
Him, her Head, then all His authority and divine power flows
through her to fulfill her purpose of being His Body here on
earth. Just as the Father was exceedingly jealous over the Son
while He lived here on earth, so now the Christ is jealous over
His Church, His betrothed Bride/wife.

The Church has been given back what Adam and Eve
lost – God's delegated authority over and in the earth. Christ,
her Head, has told her to speak in His name and "...ask
anything," and He would accomplish that which she asked
according to His will. What the Head wills, the Body executes.
As God's Ekklesia – legislative assembly – the Church is to ex-
ecute His government, as His ambassador, everywhere she is.

As in all head/body relationships, the spiritual Life-flow or
initiative, comes from the Head. Christ said His initiative came
from His Father, "The Son can do nothing of Himself, but what
He sees the Father do; for whatever He does, the Son also does
in like manner" (John 5:19, NKJV). He promised in Philippians
2:13, "for it is God who works in you both to will and to do
for His good pleasure" (NKJV). Jesus obtained authority by

being lovingly submitted to His Father, and the Church obtains authority by being lovingly submitted to Him, her Head.

Submission

In Chapter 3 we saw the perfection of the Son's submission. Now let's look at the Church's submission. This is the litmus test to prove that the Church is a living organism with a Head and a Body rightly connected to each other.

Jesus used His loving submission to the Father as proof that He was legitimately from God, and the Church can use her loving submission to prove that she is legitimately Christ's Body. Any evidence of a lack of submission becomes proof of her sin of independence and absence of true love.

We don't have to look far for convicting evidence to see a problem – perhaps just the distance to our own heart. Submission is not one of the hallmarks of the Church, especially in the western world. Several years ago a teaching spread through the Church, as if it were a new revelation, that Christ is Savior *and* Lord! The only reason it appeared to be new was because the truth of the *Lordship* of Christ had become so watered down that it was almost non-existent in certain parts of the Body of Christ. As Head, Jesus knows from His perspective that only a complete alignment of Head and Body in love can release the supernatural life-flow He intends to impart to His Body. He wants to pour Himself through that connection.

The concept of submission is as simple to understand as the connectedness and responsiveness of a physical body to its head. Concerning the body Paul wrote, "Because I am not a hand, I am not of the body?" (1Corinthians 12:15, NKJV). Can we, the body, say to the head, "Because I'm different, I'm not of you?" No! There must be oneness, and symmetry; it must flow naturally like the human body does.

We are more Greek-mind oriented, than Hebraic-heart

oriented and therefore we struggle to understand what God wants. He speaks from His heart and we hear through our minds. Our attempt to work out our faith by reason produces more independence and fear, thereby making submission a power-play struggle between God and ourselves rather than the joy it should be. Before our conversion there was an original power-play struggle for survival, for independence and a resistance to God. Post conversion, that struggle should have ended because those issues were dealt with at the Cross where it all died in Him. We are either literally redeemed or not converted at all. If we really believe He is our REDEEMER, then we can truly function in His Headship. As our Head, Jesus has commanded His Body to take up the Cross daily and follow Him in His Kingdom advance.

Too often many believe that they still possess their old histories and worldly ways of self-centeredness, rather than realize that He has bought it all, and owns it by redemption. At the same time, ironically, they expect to receive all the covenant benefits and promises of the redeemed Christian life which can only be accessed by faith in His full redemptive work. Therefore, they are missing the greatest wonder and blessing – to be one with Him.

We need to know that we have ceased being an "I" – my own god, consumed with self. Otherwise, we are functioning in a deceived, independent religious state and view God in a distorted manner: He either seems reluctant to be found, or One who expects us to perform in order to earn His favor.

He has purposed for us to become a "WE" with Him, the almighty One. His desire is that we are one in life and heart, Head and Body joined with Him. He needs to be more real to us, than anything else we know, including ourselves. His wonder, glory and power should fully manifest through us, His Body!

As leaders we need to examine what we are teaching and

modeling. The Word makes it clear that we will be accountable. Andrew Murray comments:

> I have strong fears – and I say it with all humility – that in the theology of our churches the teaching and leading of the Spirit of truth, the anointing which alone teaches all things, is not recognized in a practical sense, which a holy God demands, and which our Saviour meant Him to have. If the religious leaders of our church—teachers, pastors, Bible scholars, writers, and workers—were all fully conscious of the fact that in everything that concerns the Word of God and the church of Christ the Holy Spirit should have the supreme place of honor that He had in the church of the Acts of the Apostles, surely the signs and marks of His holy presence would be clearer and His mighty works more manifest. [4]

Jesus modeled the life of one directed by Holy Spirit – a leader, living as a dependant son, through whom the works of God were revealed. He called His disciples to follow after Him, to also walk as leaders living as dependant sons in oneness with Him.

Oneness

Herein lies the beauty and benefit of the Head/Body connection. Just as oneness with His Father caused divine life to flow through Jesus daily in every situation, so through oneness with Christ the Church can function in the divine flow of life everywhere, anytime.

It helps again to use the human body as an analogy. When we observe the beauty and wonder of a person running, hugging, studying, singing, holding a child, climbing a mountain, and so on, we see a picture of this life-connection because a head and body are one unit. Thus, the true Church with Christ as Head is full of His life – worshipping, loving, praying, evangelizing, conquering, subduing, giving, forgiving, serving, and so on. Here is the source for all authority, all loving submission and oneness. Here is all provision. There is no lack or want.

> "...And He has put all things under His feet and has made Him the head <u>over all things for the church</u>, **which is His body, <u>the fullness of Him who fills all in all</u>**" (Ephesians 1: 22 & 23, NRSV, underlining and Bold added)

Fullness, in eternal outpouring! More than we can ever dream or imagine! Fullness, greater than Niagara Falls! More expansive than all the galaxies combined! **INFINITELY F U L L!**
Holman Bible Dictionary defines this fullness as:

> *Fullness:* Completeness or totality. "The earth is the Lord's, and the fullness thereof" (Ps. 24:1). Scripture sees that nothing is really complete until it serves the purpose for which God has created it. Thus Ephesians 1:23 (NRSV) speaks of God as "him who fills all in all." *He is the one who gives everything its ultimate significance and richness. This fullness is most clearly expressed in Jesus Christ* (Col. 1:19; 2:9) from whom all true believers receive the divine life of fullness (John 1:16; 10:10). It is a life full of joy (John 15:11) and peace despite the fact of tribulations in this world (John 16:33). (Bold added).

This comment then links to eternal life. Here are some excerpts from that presentation.

ETERNAL LIFE The quality of life including the promise of resurrection which God gives to those who believe in Christ. This important term in the New Testament is emphasized in the Gospel of John, but also appears in the other Gospels and in Paul's writings. Eternal life in the New Testament eliminates the boundary line of death. Death is still a foe, but the one who has eternal life already experiences the kind of existence that will never end.

Yet in this expression, the emphasis is on the *quality* of life rather than on the unending duration of life. Probably some aspects of both quality and duration appear in every context, but some refer primarily to *quality of life* and others point to *unending life* or a *life to be entered into* in the future.

"Quality of life" involves (1) life imparted by God; (2) transformation and renewal of life; (3) life fully opened to God and centered in Him; (4) a constant overcoming of sin and moral evil; and (5) the complete removal of moral evil from the person and from the environment of that person. [5] (Bold added)

The purpose of this oneness is for us to experience the supernatural life that flows from His divine life within. We are either tapped into that source of divine life or we are not. The quality of supernatural life which we experience demonstrates to what degree we are receiving the divine flow of God's life within us. That flow of life happens individually and corporately.

1. Individually: When we are "born of the Spirit" (redeemed), then we become candidates for a continuous flow of divine supernatural life from God and we become the "well-watered garden" mentioned in Isaiah 58:11. This has happened in my own life and in the lives of millions of others. We were deserts – empty and barren – until the water of divine life began to flow, bringing an eruption of life, like a beautiful garden springing up in the desert after a rain. We bloom in His life-flow and love. As long as we do not offend or disturb that connection we are alive in Him with all His lovely nature and attributes. His life in us will accomplish everything: "…as His divine power has given to us all things that pertain to life and godliness, through the knowledge of Him who called us by glory and virtue," (2 Peter 1:3, NKJV).

2. Corporately: The flow increases as the "various members" (see 1 Corinthians 12) function corporately. Resurrection life and the power of Christ work through His corporate Body more abundantly than through individuals. This multiplies His dominion authority through us. We see the first surge of that powerful life-flow at Pentecost when Peter and the others, as His Body, respond immediately and begin to function under the direction of the Head. The resurrected Christ's life entered into them through Holy Spirit, who is the Spirit of Christ, and did through them what He had done personally while living here. People were amazed and transformed.

The Book of Acts and the rest of the New Testament are like a video of the early stages of that Life-flow: the dead were raised; people were converted; the enemy was defeated; healings abounded; people were cared for physically and spiritually; the world was transformed and the Church even rejoiced in martyrdom. The life-flow testified to the presence of Christ's headship.

The issues of love and care are without limit, either individually or corporately. What would this Christ withhold? Nothing! And His Bride/Body in turn is also to withhold nothing. Theirs is to be a love song, in harmony, each pouring their best out at the feet of the other. It is that divine love in action which the Bible says will convince the world of God's reality. We are His Body: His hands, feet, mouth, heart, eyes, ears, making Him visible, touchable, and audible, just as He was the Father's Body making the Father visible, touchable and audible. The world sees and hears Him through you and me to the degree in which we function, and honor His headship. The purposes of God's Kingdom can only be accomplished on earth by His Body lovingly responding to Him as Head.

This Holy Marriage of Christ and His Bride is the light that illuminates the next and last level of headship.

Endnotes

1. *Holman Bible Dictionary*, Quick Verse Bible Software.
2. *Funk & Wagnall's, Funk & Wagnall's Inc, New York, 1977*
3. *Spirit of Christ.* Andrew Murray. Bethany Fellowship Inc., 6820 Auto Club Rd, Minneapolis, Minnesota, 55438. 1979. Page 40.
4. *Spirit of Christ.* Andrew Murray. Bethany Fellowship Inc., 6820 Auto Club Rd, Minneapolis, Minnesota, 55438. 1979. Page 7.
5. *Holman Bible Dictionary*, Quick Verse Bible Software.

Chapter 6

THE HEAD AND BODY OF MARRIAGE

Now we come to the third level of headship: "<u>and the husband (man) is the head of his wife (woman)</u>" (1 Corinthians 11:3, NRSV, extra words and underlining mine).

This verse contains God's Kingdom order for Christian marriages and families – an order that brings the wonder and power of the other two levels of headship into their homes. In the bright light of that wonder we need to exercise some caution. Due to the history of controversy concerning headship in the home, it is necessary to keep a careful focus on its connection to the other two levels.

God is a God of order. We see that in many spectrums. The planetary systems follow the patterns God assigned them at creation: there would not be a space program if it weren't so. Animal and seed must bear after their own kind. Simply put, goats don't produce chickens, and when corn is planted, apples don't grow. We can count on that. Seasons follow seasons according to the original pattern; they don't confuse their sequence: fall doesn't come after winter. In a similar manner, marriage works better when we find God's order and function within it.

God's order and consistent purpose for headship doesn't change at the level of Christian marriage. The only difference here is that both parts, head and body, are human. On the other two levels, we observed a direct partnership with God: Level 1 is Father to Son; Level 2 is the God-man to mankind (Christ and the Church / Body). Could it be possible, at the level of human involvement that God has removed Himself? No, in fact He is very present, but oftentimes is relegated to a less obvious position.

At Level 3 the roles of man and woman as husband and wife become apparent (human to human):

> Be subject to one another out of reverence for Christ. Wives, be subject to your husbands <u>as you are to the Lord</u>. <u>For the husband is the head of the wife just as Christ is the head of the church,</u> the body of which He is the Savior. <u>Just as</u> the church is subject to Christ, <u>so also</u> wives ought to be, in everything, to their husbands. Husbands, love your wives, <u>just as</u> Christ loved the church and gave Himself up for her, in order to make her holy by cleansing her with the washing of water by the word, so as to present the church to Himself in splendor, without a spot or wrinkle or anything of the kind – yes, so that she may be holy and without blemish. <u>In the same way,</u> husbands should love their wives as they do their own bodies. He who loves his wife loves himself. For no one ever hates his own body, but he nourishes and tenderly cares for it, <u>just as</u> Christ does for the church, because we are members of his body. "For this reason a man will leave his father and mother and be joined to his wife, and the two

will become one flesh. This is a great mystery,
and I am applying it to Christ and the church.
Each of you, however, should love his wife as
himself, and a wife should respect her husband
(Ephesians 5: 21-33, NRSV, underlining mine).

In this passage Paul wrestles with "a great mystery" *(vs 32)*.
He envisions two things: the Church through marriage, and
marriage through the Church; they seem to be a mirror of and
for each other. Paul perceives both of these dimensions in a
new light. He sees the Church in a real marriage relationship
with Christ (not symbolic as some claim); he sees Christian
marriage transformed into a prototype of Christ and His Bride,
thus elevating Christian marriage from the natural realm into
the supernatural.

This level addresses God's sovereignty in our homes and
marriages and assigns value to marriage as an earthly model
and the reality of God's covenantal relationship with us. God
doesn't live in a building called a temple or church anymore;
He dwells in a living temple (us) and has the right to reign
over every aspect of our personal lives: our marriages, children,
fellowships, jobs, businesses – *everything!*

Marriage in this new Kingdom order operates in a different sphere than natural marriage. God's intention is to take up
residence with a Christian couple and to establish His Kingdom
order of headship with authority, oneness, and unity through
them. When our marriages are committed in covenant with
Him, He forms a powerful three-fold Kingdom cord.

Headship in marriage is an extension of the heavenly
umbrella over this covenantal relationship and a furtherance
of the beachhead established when Christ came to earth. This
covenant couple has the potential of manifesting the highest
level of God's authority on earth. Each family home, functioning in a godly covenantal relationship, becomes a mini-church/

ekklesia, a mini-extension of Heaven, and a bright light shining in a dark place in our communities.

Households of single Christians are also beachheads, and are not inferior, as they operate directly under Christ's headship at the second level. Singles are called to live in covenant with Christ and to be equally as bright a light in a dark place.

Marriage is a special union that God has created to manifest the deepest level of covenant possible – that of two individuals becoming one being, not just two *trying* to be one. The two are joined in a supernatural manifestation of divine oneness. Marriage is God's creation, and only His divine presence can make it work. Any married couple can attest to the fact that this special headship in the home cannot be accomplished in the natural. When a couple tries to work out a marriage on their own, they automatically institute various types of worldly order:

- a democratic system with majority rule in which everyone has the power to vote;
- a dictatorship in which someone rules according to their own preferences, with no regard as to the cost to others;
- an anarchy, with no authority at all, and everyone doing as he or she pleases.

To some degree, many couples experience these various forms of human order in their homes. Only God can make Kingdom headship and oneness possible in a marriage.

As on the other levels, headship requires God's order to exist and flourish. Let's look at authority, submission and oneness within the context of marriage.

Authority

Here we find God's authority extended to the family home. As with the other levels, in marriage there is interaction between the head and body in relation to authority.

The husband as head: What happens when an average normal, flesh and blood male is expected to be head of a marriage? Most men enter this position with little training or even knowledge, let alone experience. Many quit before they start. It shouldn't take a man long to figure out that being the head of a marriage is impossible on his own.

If he has submitted to one of the worldly systems of order in his home, such as domination, he might feel like he has things under control. But if he stands next to Father God and Christ in the line-up of headship, he will recognize that he ought to be on his knees, in humility, crying out for the miracle of Christ's grace and strength that he needs to fulfill this position as God intends.

The only hope he has of entering into true headship is by Holy Spirit, because establishing headship is a supernatural work. As the husband is rightly aligned with the other two levels of headship, the Spirit of Christ within him rises up and brings forth godly headship: authority, covering and the release of life into his home. This in turn causes the family unit to influence all spectrums that it touches, including the local church. A husband, who stands in this position, has God's backing to bring forth and maintain godly order within his home. Only then can he enforce the godly authority he needs for his marriage and family.

Through his relationship with Holy Spirit the husband needs to discern where and how to wield his authority. This authority is not for his own selfish purposes, nor is it to be surrendered to other members of the household. The husband's position as head is a high calling to establish and maintain God's

Kingdom presence at that address (the beachhead), so that his family can develop and function within it. His responsibility is to love God enough, and love his wife and family enough, to lay down his life, as Christ did for His Father and His Bride.

If we were honest, most of us would admit that we marry for selfish reasons. We want someone to take care of "ME." When that selfishness is thwarted, or challenged, we react. Headship in the home requires that the man must give up selfishness and through Holy Spirit live for his family: "..Love your wives, just as Christ also loved the church and gave Himself for her" (Ephesians 5:25, NKJV).

We read and teach this Scripture, but do we really believe it is possible? This kind of love requires humble submission and dependence on God for His divine love to shine through. On the other two levels of headship, true authority provided the heavenly umbrella of covering under which one could live the Kingdom-life here on earth. Similarly, when a married man working with Holy Spirit stands in his God-ordained role as head, a divine covering would come into place over his family.

How does this work practically? The average man wants the bottom line on what is required of him. The concept of loving a woman is easier for a man to understand if he has had healthy relationships with females, either in the role of a brother, or a good friend. In part, it involves a man's natural instinct to protect and defend "the weaker sex." For example we see Moses defending the daughters of Jethro (see Exodus 2). If a man has not been involved in healthy relationships with females, he needs God's help to understand this, because our North American culture models men in roles where they use women more often than in roles where they protect them.

Most TV programs and ads make a mockery of God's order for the home. Many actually portray the intent of demonic spirits. One ungodly spirit is Jezebel, who mocks godly authority and a man's place in his home: most males in these shows look stupid and ineffectual. Another dominant spirit is misogyny (the hatred, suppression and victimization of women) which portrays females as mindless, greedy sex objects. Little of the media, if any, demonstrate a true representation of God's truth and order.

Manly headship begins with spiritual guardianship over one's wife and children and requires diligent warfare on the home-front. A husband and father must be on alert for ungodly influences that are trying to control or spoil God's intended Kingdom atmosphere for that household. Here are some indicators to watch for:

- ungodly attitudes such as selfishness, disrespect, or callousness;
- negative influences that come from outside either through people or the media: television, video games, books, magazines or the Internet.

These indicators, as well as other daily situations, require a husband/father to exercise his headship. He must discern the cause of the problem in each situation, with the help of his wife and sometimes others, and deal with it appropriately. Identifying what is appropriate is an extensive task, but here are some suggestions:

- simple basic prayer is often sufficient;
- adding spiritual warfare in the form of binding the enemy's influence can be helpful;
- good old-fashioned discipline and correction, along with teaching, may be necessary.

At all times, a show of unity between husband and wife can prevent or settle many issues. I realize that this advice is minimal, but some valuable recommended reading can be found in the Endnotes.[1]

The wife as the body: How does authority operate for the woman in marriage?

Good news ladies! The pattern derived from the other two levels indicates that the body receives all the authority it needs to function on earth from the head. In marriage the wife is the body and her authority rests in her covenantal relationship with her husband. Authority passes down through the other levels to her. As a child of God she can align directly to Christ's headship and as a wife, she can also connect through the headship of her husband, sharing in all he receives from God.

As she partners with her husband (in head/body relationship) they become a unit. They each function in their distinctive roles as head/body, working that out in their culture and circumstances. As they walk in agreement, she can wield all the authority she needs to protect their home, their children, their business or their neighborhood. According to Genesis 3, she is hell's number one problem.

An analogy would be of a mother lion taking care of her cubs. Few predators bother her family while she is on guard. Similarly, the Proverbs 31 woman cares for her household. Her family is well fed and clothed. She knows in her heart she has godly authority to go forth and prosper because her husband blesses her. She is *for* him, and not *against* him. He is *for* her, and delights in her success. He is not intimidated by her. The more prosperous she becomes, the more he is pleased. She respects and honors her husband both within and outside the home. Together they are the pipeline of God's blessings to their children and to society.

According to God's order, a husband's primary assignment is to love his wife, and a wife's primary assignment is to respect her husband. Evidently God knows each gender's weaknesses and struggles.

A woman can have difficulty respecting her husband. Her

inclination is to withhold respect until she sees a high level of performance. She also tends toward control and may take over when she perceives failure. Many women try to mother their husbands and can't figure out why they act like boys. Women need to see their husbands through God's eyes as their head and to encourage (not force or berate) them to trust God to establish divine headship through them.

Let me say at this point that I am not trying to promote human idealism as something separated from real life. Anyone who is married knows that pretending to live in a fantasy of having an ideal married life, is just as unrealistic as pretending to live in a fantasy of perfect religious Christianity, without exhibiting any negative feelings or behavior. This does not negate the truth that we are capable of much more with God in our lives, than we are on our own.

Living a life under God's headship requires that we surrender our self-improvement programs at the Cross, and believe in the completed work He accomplished for us. We must function in oneness with Christ's Spirit within us, through His Blood, in order to live the life God has purposed for us. It is not about God helping "me" live my life, but about "our" living through Him the life He has determined.

Just as Christ Himself, and the Church, received their authority from their Head through submission, so the wife must also.

Submission

It says in Ephesians 5:24: "Just as the Church is subject to Christ, so let the wives be to their own husbands in everything" (NKJV, underlining mine). The same principle and process is at work in the home as in the Church. Just as the Son is the Body submitted to His Head, Father God, and just as the Church is the Body submitted to her Head Christ, so the wife is the body submitted to her head, her husband.

Our Redeemer-Husband: Our Head

The power of headship can only be experienced through willing submission based on love. The power of headship is based on *position* – that of *being* submitted – not an act or behavior of *trying* to submit. On Levels 1 and 2 submission has been a heavenly experience dependent on the supernatural flow of Holy Spirit. Two humans cannot force themselves, or each other, into a position of head and body in an attempt to make something happen. Only God, through His Spirit in us, can accomplish this submission in marriage or in any other human relationship.

The word "submit" used here derives from the Greek *hupotasso*, which translates "subject yourself." It is used again in verse 21(Eph. 5, NKJV), "submitting to one another in the fear of God". One might paraphrase it thus: be the various members of the body together, for the honor of the Head, Christ, and the benefit of the whole.

From this broader discussion of submission concerning the Body of Christ, Paul moves into the specifics of the marriage relationship and says the relationship between husband and wife is "Just as." In other words, the two are aligned into one: "…and the two will become one flesh" *(vs. 31)*. They are no longer two individuals, but now are a married covenantal unit, a beachhead on earth for the Kingdom of God. Kelly Varner says it this way:

> Prior to the fall they were one. There was
> no need for authority and submission; it was
> swallowed up in simplicity and union. In order
> for authority and submission to operate there
> must be two wills. One will must come under
> and submit to the other will. For that reason
> we see that obedience is not the ultimate goal.
> There is something greater than my submitting
> to His will. The highest order of anything is to

> become it! We are to come into union with His
> will….one will. Jesus was the pattern for this.[2]

We can illustrate this kind of unity and oneness in the example of a couple figure skating or waltzing harmoniously together, canoeing compatibly together, or enjoying synchronized swimming in perfect symmetry. For two to function together properly, there naturally must be a leader. For those viewing the couples skating, dancing, swimming or canoeing, the issue of leadership is not the focus. The beauty of the activity and how well the two perform together is what really matters. The more the couples have practiced, the more wonderful they are to watch. They blend together, and thus become one.

As we have seen, in the marriage covenant God pairs a man and a woman to merge as one through the supernatural life-flow of Holy Spirit working through two surrendered lives. It is a manifestation of divine life that only works through corporateness. A divine multiplication of life happens in corporateness that cannot function through individualism. When a man and a woman are willing to "die" to their individualism, and invite God to join them in a corporate covenant, something happens that makes them more than one-plus-one-makes-two.

Elijah House Ministries, and probably many others, teach that marriage is "designed to grind" the two partners – to rightly "kill" each one. Only as each one lays down his/her life first to Christ, and then to the other, can this head/body corporate union release the divine flow of life. Only through God is real unity and oneness possible. It takes much practice, with failures and repentance along the way, to get the rhythm of this flow and to maintain it. The rewards of perseverance leading to breakthrough and victory are priceless.

As we all know, this has been a controversial issue. The devil is afraid of God's order in the family home and the authority that covenant Kingdom relationship carries. The equation of multiplication that one puts 1000 to flight and two put 10,000 to flight really applies here. Just as the devil is warring against unity in the Church, he is also opposing unity in the home. He has produced a confusing array of teachings and religions to try to hinder corporate Christianity, and he has also successfully confused the issue of marital oneness to keep us from operating in it.

God never intended man and woman to be pitted against one another; this conflict stems from the enemy's schemes. God intended man and woman to partner and work together. He created them male and female for exactly that purpose. They are perfectly matched to function together, and when they do so through Him, then all the benefits of oneness are manifest on this level.

Oneness

As on the previous two levels, oneness releases all the life-flow necessary to live, all the authority, and all the unity that the wife needs as the body. There is a continuum of life-flow from Level 1, through Level 2, and on to Level 3, with Christ in the center of it all.

Everything that the husband needs in order to function as the head, and everything the wife needs to enable her as the body, comes through their oneness in Christ. Just as symmetry and total unity are necessary within the human body between the head and body, so must a married couple be united as one for God's life to flow and manifest. Their mutual submission to oneness activates the power to function together. For her, it is the power to submit – to be joined without rebellion or fear. For him, it is the strength and courage to lovingly stand for God in his home without selfishness or anger. They both need the ability to trust God in this new life form, so that two can be as one.

The fruitfulness of oneness is found in the divine unity of marriage as it was with the other levels (provision, love and care). God has given clear directives concerning that care:

> Husbands, go all out in your love for your wives, exactly as Christ did for the church – a love marked with giving, not getting. Christ's love makes the church whole. His words evoke her beauty. Everything he does and says is designed to bring the best out of her, dressing her in dazzling white silk, radiant with holiness. And that is how husbands ought to love their wives. They are really doing themselves a favor – since they are already "one" in marriage (Ephesians 5: 28, 29, The Message).

It is not that God cares more for the body than for the head. Each has its part to fulfill. The husband's part is to care for his wife, his body. He is even warned that unloving treatment of her will hinder his prayers. She is his "glory" (see 1 Corinthians 11:15), as Christ the Son is the Father's glory (see Hebrews 1:3).

The Proverbs 31 woman thrived in her union with her husband as his glory and they both were blessed. She functioned within their social position, was treated as an extension of him and thus had authority to buy goods and land in that day. She blossomed in her husband's love and support.

Unless the wife (the body) is cared for, she will not be able to be her husband's (the head's) glory. She is like a plant that responds to proper care and flourishes accordingly.

Women are created to be life-givers. When they feel loved and cared for, that life-giving gift is released and flows, provided it has not been badly damaged. It benefits her husband, children and extended family, both natural and spiritual. As the body of their covenant for the home, she is responsible for the life - flow being tangible in their relationship, as well as to family members, and to others near them.

This divine pattern for marriage may look and function differently from home to home due to various cultures and personalities, but the headship order and principles remain steadfast. God set these realities concerning men and women in place in the Garden of Eden, and they really haven't changed. Adam and Eve's original rebellion didn't destroy that order, but introduced some new variables into it.

Before Adam and Eve sinned they were in unity and covenant with God. When they acted independently against Him, He had to establish some new boundaries and had to relate differently to them. When Christ accomplished His work of a new Blood-covenant on the Cross, only then through His resurrection and ascension, could the broken relationship with God and with each other be restored and His divine order re-established.

When we are out of God's order, discord and disunity exist. Over many years, and in many different types of living situations, I have heard a common "song" sung by married couples. The man chants, "She won't let me lead; she doesn't respect me; she's independent." The woman rehearses, "He doesn't love me, therefore I can't/won't yield to him; he's selfish and will use me." When this "singing" couple is presented with the biblical ideal of harmony through oneness, fear and frustration result.

After reading an earlier draft of this book, a friend of mine responded in anger which was a surprise to me. His anger was based on a deep-rooted frustration concerning his role as head of his home; yet to me, he appeared to be a happily, married, Christian man. It was obvious that this couple had been "singing the song" of discord. They exemplified marriage partners who had become frustrated and tired because they had not yet entered into the godly headship designed for them.

Once again, I'm not promoting humanistic utopia in marriage, but because everything works better according to God's order, I believe the biblical issue of headship would help make Christian marriage a blessed state.

The Bible uses the analogy of the human body to help us understand how the Body of Christ functions. God's order is quite evident in the human body. This scriptural analogy can therefore help us with deeper insights of Body-life, both for the Church, and for marriage relationships as well.

Endnotes

1. Suggested Readings
   a) *Wild at Heart*. John Eldridge. Thomas Nelson LTD Publishers. 2001
   Eldridge also suggested *Treat Her Right*. Roy Head and Gene Kurtz. (No info)
   b) *Marketplace, Marriage and Revival*. Jack Serra. Longwood Communications, 3037 Clubview Drive, Orlando 2001.
2. *The Priesthood is Changing*. Kelly Varner. Destiny Image Publishers Inc. P.O. Box 351, Shippensburg, PA.,17257-0315. 1991. Page 73.

Chapter 7
THE PHYSICAL HEAD AND BODY

A comparison of the human body with its many parts to the Body of Christ and to the marriage relation-ship, can yield insight into various aspects of how a body, and the life within a body, function. From this analogy we can delve deeper into the relationship between the head and body. Examination of the various systems of the physical body will reveal their interdependence and symmetry. It will be helpful to compare how the primary issues of health and life are expressed in a body both physically and spiritually.

God in His infinite mercy has given us pictures to help us understand His meaning when He refers to the Kingdom and to the Church. The various analogies for the Body used in the Scriptures (referred to in Chapter 1), give us a broad, varied picture of the Church, while an individual picture, like the one of the human body, gives us an opportunity to look closer at body related issues.

Paul introduces the comparison of the human body to the Body of Christ in 1 Corinthians 12:

> Now there are <u>varieties of gifts</u>, but the same
> Spirit; and there are varieties of services, but the

same Lord; and there are <u>varieties of activities,</u> but it is the same God who activates all of them in everyone. To each is given the manifestation of the Spirit for the common good.

To one is given through the Spirit.... All these are activated by one and the same Spirit, who allots to each one individually just as the Spirit chooses. For just as the body is one and has <u>many members</u>, and all the members of the body, <u>though many, are one body</u>, so it is with Christ. <u>For in the one Spirit we were all baptized into one body</u>—Jews or Greeks, slaves or free--and we were all made to drink of one Spirit. Indeed, the body does not consist of one member but of many. If the foot would say... And if the ear would say....If the whole body were an eye....

But as it is, God arranged the members in the body, each one of them, as he chose. If all were a single member, where would the body be? As it is, there are many members, yet one body. The eye cannot say to the hand, ... On the contrary, the members of the body that seem to be weaker are indispensable, and those members of the body that we think less honorable we clothe with greater honor, and our less respectable members are treated with greater respect; whereas our more respectable members do not need this.

But God has so arranged the body, giving the greater honor to the inferior member, that there may be no dissension within the body, but the members may have the same care for one another. If one member suffers.... <u>Now you are the Body of Christ and individually members of it.</u> (1 Corinthians 12: 4-8a, 11-27, NRSV, underlining mine).

Even with a general knowledge of anatomy, this picture is quite clear. God is comparing our physical body with the Body of Christ. This comparison of bodies can be understood externally, merely in referring to our hands and feet along with our limbs, torso and head, or can involve the internal complexity of our "many members". Whichever way we compare these bodies, we have much to learn. An overview of the structure of the human body may be helpful to this process.

Within the composite that we call the human body, 11 systems are at work. These systems take care of life with its various demands:

- **The cardiovascular system** includes blood, heart, arteries, veins and capillaries.
- **The digestive system** begins at the mouth and ends at the colon, consisting of the esophagus, stomach and small and large intestines.
- **The skeletal system and the muscular system** are comprised of bones, muscles, ligaments and joints.
- **The nervous system** encompasses the brain and spinal cord with miles of nerve fiber and connectors throughout the whole body.
- **The endocrine system** is made up of a collection of hormone - producing glands and cells.

There are also the **respiratory, reproductive, urinary, lymphatic and tissue systems.** Each is unique and has many fascinating and awesome intricacies. I plan to write a companion book to this one that explores these systems and examines how they parallel the systems within the Church.

Each unique system is a state of the art wonder, but yet is interrelated and inter-dependent. Because the body is corporate, each has a part to play in the corporate life-flow. Neither the head nor body, along with its systems, has life without corporateness. All cells function corporately, and if any function independently, then diseases such as cancer develop.

How bizarre it would seem for one part of our body to attempt to function alone! What would happen to the rest of the body if an eye decided it was bored helping with its gift of sight and freelanced, without care? Abundant life exists for the whole body only when each system functions properly as God created it to function, in co-operation with the others. All systems must be inter-connected for an interchange of what they need from each other. For example, the heart has its own electrical panel, and any interruption of the electrical current which comes through the nervous system would stop its muscles from pumping. Blood supplied by the heart and needed by all other systems, would cease to flow.

Another illustration is that of the brain, the command center. It also is dependent on the other systems; any interruption to its supply of oxygen through the blood would cause serious damage.

Within the physical body we find the interplay of authority and life. The brain is the command center and therefore represents authority – the head. Several things become obvious as we examine the physical inter-relationship of the head and the body. They give us tools with which to measure the health of the spiritual head/body relationship.

Here are some obvious, critical aspects of this head/body relationship:

- **There has to be life within the brain**. One can have a perfect physical body, but if the brain ceases to function, it doesn't matter how good the body is.

The head, with its brain, orchestrates the life-flow for the rest of the body.

- **The converse is true: the body must be fit and responsive** to the brain's commands or its parts are ineffective. A paralyzed or broken arm cannot move no matter how the brain directs it.
- **The head and body are interdependent on each other**, each with its own responsibility. The head directs, and the body responds. One without the other is useless or deformed.

We all admire the human body when it functions well, especially in sports, the arts, and in advertising. Our culture spends a great deal of time watching the human body perform. If the head and body are properly aligned, primary, positive evidences of life are apparent:

- symmetry and order exist (unity);
- productivity and beauty are evident;
- satisfaction and delight are felt;
- ongoing and increasing life is manifest.

However, not everything about this body-life is positive. It can have a negative side. In our youthful years we take our bodies for granted and expect them to respond the way we require. As we age they complain and rebel, often refusing to co-operate quickly. Due to accidents or illness, some people lose their physical abilities at an earlier age. When the natural head and body are not properly connected, there are obvious negative symptoms. The common ones are:

- disorder and disunity among members (*dissension*);
- erratic functioning and poor productivity;
- irritation and frustration;

- separation and death.

These negative symptoms are a key to identifying or diagnosing possible health problems. They also help to determine proper intervention and resolution of the issues in order to prevent death.

One can examine any living thing, just as the human body is able to be examined and assessed for signs and symptoms of health or disease. The standards for health are applicable as a guide to evaluate other areas of life. Signs and symptoms are clues that direct us to an accurate diagnosis.

Are any of the above negative signs and symptoms found in the three levels of headship? Let's examine each level.

Level 1: Heavenly Father and Son

There are no negative symptoms here, but there could have been if Jesus had not fully submitted. If He, as the Body, had acted independently of His Head, there would be no new covenant, no salvation, no Holy Spirit to live in us. Hence, we see the reason why Satan tried so hard to tempt Him to act independently, to break the connection with His Head, especially during His 40 days in the desert.

Level 2. Christ and the Church

Both positive and negative symptoms are obvious here: all negative ones originate in the Church. It is grievous to admit, but these are common:

- disorder and disunity among members, both individual and corporate;
- erratic functioning and poor productivity;
- irritation and frustration;

- separation (church splits) and death.

Therefore one can rightly diagnose that there are serious problems within the Head/Body connection on this level. The enemy has been busy here, tempting the Body to act independently of her Head. Satan knows that when he can accomplish independence and disunity, then the full flow of life from God is disrupted and there is less chance of his work and plans being thwarted. The resulting symptoms are obvious, and we are guilty of independence and rebellion: of trying to be a god ourselves.

Since the life-flow and healthy relationship between the physical head and the body is the key proponent of a basic normal life for any of us, any disruption, accident or illness, affecting that connection, produces many problems. We are not only physical beings, but a delicate balance of spirit, soul and body. Discord and disruption on any level can affect our physical lives.

It is well known that many in the Church are ill and some die prematurely. When we combine those medical statistics with the fact that a very low percentage of divine healings occurs in North America, we have to conclude we are experiencing definite signs and symptoms of a serious disconnectedness between Head and Body.

Level 3. Husband and wife

Statistics reveal copious negative symptoms at this level. Happy marriages seem to be a rarity. The diagnosis indicates serious trouble:

- disorder and disunity among family members;
- erratic functioning and poor productivity;
- irritation and frustration;

- separation and death (that is divorce).

The fruit of these symptoms becomes most obvious in the children of these marriages: they are hurting, frustrated, disconnected, and lonely. It seems clear that there are serious problems with the Head/Body connection due to the enemy's schemes to produce independent behavior. His motives are revealed in John 10:10: "The thief comes only to steal and kill and destroy" (NRSV). The enemy wants to keep the Head and the Body apart, thereby cutting off the life-flow intended to nurture that frontline family home, so that it can't shine brightly as a beachhead beacon.

God has used this human body analogy to give us the pictures that we need for a deeper understanding of the Head/Body relationship. "….many members…one body…" In causing many members to work together (Ephesians 5), God created a higher life-order that is a spiritual Body. This is true both of the Church and of marriage and reveals God's life at work in us. How God works this transformation extends beyond human reason into the supernatural because it is Heaven's life manifest in the world.

The new spiritual Body, the Church, formed from the seed – Jesus – continues to grow as His life is spread abroad into our hearts bringing forth many "sons" or members, and thus potentially the Bride. This sonship is for both men and women and refers to our being joint-heirs with Christ: "Now if we are children, then we are heirs – heirs of God and co-heirs with Christ, if indeed we share in His sufferings in order that we may also share in His glory" (Romans 8:17, NIV). This sharing is about that covenantal oneness with Him.

Many still believe the lie that we have to earn sonship and that it is hard to obtain, but the truth is Christ has done all that was necessary for us to enter into our inheritance with and in Him. Our blood-bought redemption is a complete deal.

Nothing more is needed to make us one with Him. Sanctification is the process of our growing up from spiritual childhood into full sonship in Him, similar to our human development.

This negative fruit of *disorder* within the Body is very serious, whether in the home relationship where it brings "illness and death" into the heart of the family, or within the Body of Christ where it brings spiritual and physical death; it must be identified and dealt with. The divine life-flow intended by God must be restored.

When we are established in a deeper, fuller, truer revelation of the connection with Christ and His headship both personally and corporately, we will be healthier both spiritually and physically, and our witness and prayers will be filled with power and authority.

Chapter 8
HISTORY AND REVELATION

There is no question that Christ has a Body here on earth. Our issues are: How healthy is His Body? How corporate is His Body? Does it demonstrate the full connection of Head and Body? Is Christ able to orchestrate everything He desires through His Body on earth, or are there hindrances? How is the expansion of the beachhead progressing? Since we have concluded that there are problems, we have to look at the Church's history to find the root causes.

History taking is an important aspect of accurate diagnosing. Whether the body is physical or spiritual, it will have a history because all living things have history which can help us understand the cause and the cure for the problems. These negative symptoms began to develop a long time ago as we find Paul writing strong words to the churches about such issues:

- "Now in giving these instructions I do not praise you, since you come together not for the better but for the worse" (1 Corinthians 11:17, NKJV).
- "So I tell you this, and insist on it in the Lord, that you must no longer live as the Gentiles do, in the futility of their thinking" (Ephesians 4:17, NIV).

Christ Himself delivered some stinging reproaches to the churches:

- "Yet I hold this against you: You have forsaken your first love. Remember the height from which you have fallen! Repent and do the things you did at first. If you do not repent, I will come to you and remove your lampstand from its place" (Revelation 2:4,5, NIV).
- "But I have a few things against you: you have some there who hold to the teaching of Balaam, who taught Balak to put a stumbling block before the people of Israel, so that they would eat food sacrificed to idols and practice fornication. So you also have some who hold to the teaching of the Nicolaitans. Repent then. If not, I will come to you soon and make war against them with the sword of my mouth" (Revelation 2:14-16, NRSV). (all above underlining mine)

Many influences came against the new Church: Judaism (the former ways), Mithraism (false saviour), Gnosticism (special knowledge), Nicolaitans (deception that physical sin does not defile spiritual purity), Paganism (heathenism in its various forms), the teaching of Baalam (compromise), and other heresies. Jim Chosa enlarges upon this aspect:

Apart from the spiritual help of the Holy Spirit, the issue of good and evil becomes soul-based, and sets the stage for man through democratic means to begin to set up religious caste systems where certain men have greater influence and power over others. Democracy as a political form of government is honorable, but as a form of government in the Body of Christ is de-

94

plorable since it replaces the Head of the Body, Jesus Christ, with majority rule. This is the root purpose of the power of humanism! If we are to study humanism through history, we would see the message," ye shall be gods," as a driving force of man becoming the center of all things. For western Christianity, Satan set up an elaborate trap using as bait the three humanistic Greek pillars of philosophy: Epicureanism, Stoicism, and Gnosticism.

Gnosticism is based on crude notions of the spiritual and material world, and labels all things material or natural as being evil including man's soul and body. Included is a strange doctrine of a seven-fold evil separation of Earth from Heaven. Epicureanism taught man's goals should be a life of pleasure regulated by morality, temperance, serenity, and cultural development. Stoicism believed all happenings are the result of divine will and, therefore, man should be calmly accepting of this will, and free from passion, grief and joy. In other words, my life is controlled by fate, and there is nothing I can do about it so why try. All three are soul based, and meant to confine man through the perversion of his mind to the soul and material realm only. If I believe any of these false beliefs, why should I try and gain freedom through prayer and spiritual warfare since the way it is, is as free as it gets. [1]

The apostles and early Church family fought the good fight to keep these influences from destroying the truths which Christ had laid as a foundation. They knew that the supernatural life of God being released through Holy Spirit to the Body of Christ was under attack by the beguiler. It had to be guarded and nurtured.

Historically there have been other negative influences:

- Constantine made Christianity the state religion of the Roman Empire and began to interfere in its governance.
- A major shift from heart to mind happened; when the Hebraic heart-based life was purposely eliminated from the Church, Greek philosophy and a Roman rulership-style moved to the forefront.
- The above shift introduced an emphasis on individualism and reasoning, instead of on the unified family God had intended for His Body to be.
- Political maneuvers created and maintained seats of power in the developing Roman religious structure, thus resulting in a religious Empire, with an Emperor.
- The pagans of the Roman Empire were suddenly forced to be in the Roman Christian church without the necessary internal change of salvation. They brought with them pagan symbols, festivities, and practices, many of which are still operating in the Church today.
- Various non-biblical teachings arose, such as the idea that the gifts and the power of Holy Spirit were only for the early Church and not necessarily for the modern age. This greatly hindered Holy Spirit's work.
- There developed a separate group called clergy and a controlled admission to that position. This divided the Body and created a hierarchical system with the position of clergy reserved only for men, thus separating God's team.
- Obligatory celibacy for male clergy was mandated– a potentially unhealthy lifestyle, the fruit of which is evidenced in some recent news stories further dividing the purposed, unified family of God.

Rick Joyner says this about Church history:

> After the cutting edge move of the Holy Spirit departed from Antioch, the apostolic ministry actually faded out. A few centuries later, prophets were no longer recognized. The evangelists were replaced by politics and the sword as the leaders of the church sought to take the world for Christ by might and power rather than by the Spirit. The teachers and pastors were displaced by priests who basically reduced Christianity to rituals in place of faith. This led to what many historians call the Dark Ages.[2]

Although God has faithfully kept a remnant of His Church (His seed), alive and functioning on earth, these negative issues have greatly influenced the development of the majority of the Church as we know it. Many deviations and substitutes have entered her, including the one under consideration in this book.

Diagnostic history-taking has revealed many causes of the problems we have identified. The core problem relates to headship. Throughout this book I have been establishing the groundwork in order to share with you the revelation of headship that I believe is representative of God's heart for Christ's Body. We have examined various aspects of headship and some conclusions bear emphasizing:

- **God is a God of order:** all He brings forth, either spiritual or natural, bears the evidence of His divine order.
- **Headship is His plan:** He established and initiated it Himself.
- **Headship is about relationship:** it involves *being*, not *doing*.

- **Headship is a primary element** of His Kingdom purposes here on earth.
- **Headship is the supernatural life-flow** that brings God's presence to earth and establishes all the authority, and power to fulfill His purposes here.
- **Headship emerges from God's heart** and is manifest on earth through the three levels we have discussed. These levels establish the cornerstones of God's Kingdom here on earth.

Each of the three levels of headship has distinct assignments:

- **Level 1** established Christ's glorious beachhead victory on earth through His love and submission. The power of the Cross and the Blood destroyed the power of the evil one, thus setting in place the cornerstone for God's Kingdom rule on earth.
- **Level 2** vastly expanded the beachhead of the Kingdom, throughout the cities and nations of the world as His Church spread.
- **Level 3** established the beachhead in every Christian family and within a covenant of marriage that make it possible for each neighborhood to be represented. The assignments of husband and wife function fully, though somewhat differently, through the supernatural life flowing from the head to the body, connecting from level to level.

Because the revelation that I want to share is primarily based on Level 2, we need to examine it in more depth.

As the Head of the Church and her husband, Christ has certain wishes and desires for His betrothed Wife:

- He wants to be her Head and to see the fullness of His divine, supernatural life, imparted in and through her;
- He wants to cover her with His authority and protect her;
- He wants to love, cherish and care for her;
- He wants to work with her to fulfill His Kingdom mandate.

Like all husbands, He desires that His Bride would look to Him for all her intimacy needs. He does not want her seeking elsewhere for what He alone is called to give her. There is a grief and jealousy in any husband who knows that he is not his wife's best friend and confidant and that she has looked to another. God called Israel a harlot over and over again because she kept looking to others – to the pagan peoples and their gods – for what He alone wanted to give to her.

Christ's heart today for His Bride and Church carries the same jealousy. Like a natural husband, He feels desire and passion for His Bride. Natural husbands may struggle with a sense of inadequacy to meet the bride's needs, but not this divine husband. He is without limit. He is assured within Himself that He is more than able to meet all her needs. A natural husband may push his wife away in frustration, but this supernatural husband will never do that. Christ stands before His Bride in His *fullness*, wanting her to draw from His life.

The River of Life flowing from Him is for her. He died for her, paid all her debts and healed her wounds. He has done everything necessary to bring Himself and His Church together as one. He has removed the curse of sin and separation through His sacrifice of love. He then departed from His Bride's presence, so that He could release Holy Spirit to come in order to unite her with Himself thus making her one in divine essence and life-flow:

> Blessed be the God and Father of our Lord Jesus Christ, who has blessed us with every spiritual blessing in the heavenly places in Christ, just as He chose us in Him before the foundation of the world, that we should be holy and without blame before Him in love, having predestined us to adoption as sons by Jesus Christ to Himself, according to the good pleasure of His will, to the praise of the glory of His grace, by which He made us accepted in the Beloved (Ephesians 1:3-6, NKJV).

The Church is *betrothed* to Christ, which means married to Him, not just engaged. Jewish betrothal was a legal covenant with traditional requirements that needed fulfillment before it became legally binding. All parties had to be in agreement concerning the desired bride and the bride price negotiated and paid. A legal contract / covenant was signed. Finally a covenant cup was shared by each of the prospective marriage partners: first by the bride as an acceptance of him in marriage, and then by the groom to legally seal forever the betrothal covenant between them.

Once these steps were completed, the couple was legally bound to fulfill their marriage commitment to one another. The betrothed husband was released to go to prepare a place for his bride – usually an extension of his father's house. When the father knew all was ready, he released the waiting husband to begin the wedding processional and banquet, thus completing their marriage covenant. As with Mary and Joseph, because they were betrothed, had he not wanted to accept her child, he would have had to divorce or stone her.

This is the glorious reality that God set in motion for and through His Son. All of God and His resources are available to the betrothed Bride as she prepares herself for the coming day of the marriage feast of the Lamb. Is this glory a living reality in the Church as we know it? Is Christ's Body His alone? Is their love affair the heart-pounding reality of her existence? Are we one Bride preparing for her Beloved, or are we divided and segregated? (God doesn't have a harem.)

Are there beliefs and structures within the Church that defy the fullness of His love and authority? Personally I've encountered a few:

- Love is considered emotional, and feminine; therefore it is dangerous and suspect. We prefer emphasizing duty and ministry.
- Only men have been called to spiritual authority and pulpit ministry.
- Only those who are trained professionals are to minister.
- Women should engage in the service-oriented ministry of children's work and kitchen duty.
- Women are not to teach men, though they can teach boys who are more vulnerable to deception.
- The head of the local church is the senior pastor and/or the board.
- The Body is organized by gender in a pyramid structure: men are at the top, and women below them. Men can progress to leadership positions from the bottom to the top, as on a corporate business ladder, but women are restricted in their leadership potential.
- The congregation should be content to sit quietly week after week being preached at, while the lost and poor do not receive the preaching that Christ intended for them: "to preach good news to the poor" (Isaiah 61:1, NIV).

These are just some existing practices. The list can be ex-

101

panded or contracted. Since we are responsible for working out our theology with "fear and trembling," I have been attempting to do my homework. These differing perspectives have caused me to inquire of God concerning His point of view.

I have, however, encountered hindrances and risks along the way. For instance, most of the time I have been too busy with ongoing activities and responsibilities of various aspects of Kingdom work to pursue this study ardently. I am aware of the possible risks of being perceived as cultish, of being accused of heresy, or of getting painted as an extremist, liberal, or fanatic.

What lies at the root of these issues? The divine revelation that I have received has shed considerable light on these. It concerns a significant substitution that has infiltrated the Church almost unbeknownst to the Body of Christ because it confuses understanding of headship roles. It is a twist of God's original design for headship and therefore seems familiar. The compromise has occurred between Level 2 and Level 3 of God's headship structure. Both are husband/wife structures.

The twistedness is simply this: **the headship order of the home,** that of a husband (man) being head of his wife (woman) **has wrongly replaced Christ's headship of the Church.** Men are expected to have authority and be in leadership, while women are expected to be subject or submissive to them.

The roles of men and women have become a dominant issue while the true headship of Christ has become secondary. This confusion is presented as God's own plan and order while in God's eyes it creates major disorder. The true headship of Christ is replaced by a lesser form of headship. God's Level 3 design for husband and wife has become confused with God's Level 2 design for Christ as Head with the Church. Level 2 concerns spiritual marriage while Level 3 concerns human marriage. Christ's Bride includes every man, woman and child: "many members....one body" (Ephesians 5) with no internal division.

This particular compromise has been added to the original one of man trying to be a god. That struggle had been in the Church and culminated in Constantine's time when Roman rule was introduced with all its hierarchy, followed by gender division, along with the separation of the clergy and the congregation.

As this confused compromise has gained more control within the Church, it has re-structured God's original plan and design and has constricted Holy Spirit's supernatural life-flow creating a vacuum that has allowed this compromise and variations of it to flourish. It crept into the Church by a gradual process over the centuries through different events and stages. That is generally how the enemy works. He infiltrates, undercover, through subtle compromises with the ultimate goal of gaining control.

Proof that this twisted substitution exists is not hard to find. We need only identify Christian congregations and (or) organizations that promote separation of Christ's Body along gender lines. Other unbiblical divisions can include ethnicity, education or social structure. Such segregations should not exist within the Church of Christ:

> ... for in Christ Jesus you are all children of God through faith. As many of you as were baptized into Christ have clothed yourselves with Christ. There is no longer Jew or Greek, there is no longer slave or free, there is no longer male and female; for all of you are one in Christ Jesus. And if you belong to Christ, then you are Abraham's offspring, heirs according to the promise (Galatians 3:26 –29, NRSV, underlining mine).

These variances still exist within our natural social structures: a Jew is still a Jew; a master is a master; and a male is a male. Scripture does not imply that we should eliminate these natural identities. It refers to spiritual truths and issues to do with God's Kingdom people who transcend beyond these natural identities, because they are spiritually born again of Him, both male and female, in relationship with Christ. These identities and differences are supposed to be in submission to His identity thereby manifesting His unity in His Body. The more we emphasize these natural identities – our gender, our nationality, our age group, our occupation, and our education – the more we thwart the unity and oneness of His Body.

Household headship functioning within the Church produces undesirable fruit:

- wrongful control by humans over the people within the Church;
- distortion of the full unity of both males and females with Christ;
- lack of full body functioning, but controlled by human rules determining who can function where and when;
- human organizational methods used to manage the Church;
- gender confusion and stress;
- authority confusion, stress and resentment;
- children relegated to a baby form of Church.

Though not all congregations experience these issues, they are quite common. They have been accepted as part of a theological package bolstered by certain Scriptures, while the glaring reality that the Church is not focused on Christ, remains obscured.

Some congregations are far less affected by such compromise. It is a delight and refreshing to participate with them, because they trust Holy Spirit's flow through whomsoever and however He chooses. Such leaderships release the whole local body to be Kingdom citizens, whether in church services, at home, or at work. This is more evident in the present apostolic season as apostolic churches, ministries, businesses and governments are emerging. Thank God a fresh move of His Spirit around the world is bringing the Church back to her first love to lay true foundations for the next stage of His Kingdom plans!

In summary, God is very creative in His design of living structures with reference both to the human body and to the Church. He would only create a Church that demonstrates His governmental order. From the beginning His Church has had elders, and leaders along with apostles, prophets, evangelists, pastors and teachers.

As in the human body, certain organs occupy leadership roles within the whole structure. An example in the human body of an organ assigned a leadership role is the heart, which leads the vascular system. Another would be the lungs, which are the primary members of the respiratory system, or the brain, which commands the neurological system.

In the Church, the leaders whom God has ordained are not meant to replace Christ as the Head. Holy Spirit works through them, and through every member of the local body to encourage and guide the Church's development and life. Leaders can exhort and encourage, but they are never to own or control. We see them in the New Testament, at every important junction, praying and fasting over and over again to seek direction from God. Christ told His followers to wait for Holy Spirit who would guide them. In other words, do not trust in your own understanding, (paraphrase of Proverbs 3:5).

What are the effects of this substitution on God (Father, Son and Spirit), the Church, and men and women? We will explore this in the next chapter.

Endnotes

1. Jim & Faith Chosa, *Thy Kingdom Come Thy Will Be Done In Earth*, Day Chief Ministries Inc: 2004, Page 181.
2. Rick Joyner, *Shadows of Things to Come,* Thomas Nelson Publishers, Nashville, Tennessee. 1958, Page 69-70

Chapter 9

SUBSTITUTION'S FRUIT

To discern the effects of substituting the headship of marriage for the headship of Christ over His Church, the first question to ask is, what does God think about it? Does He mind? How does it affect Him, and His purposes?

Many Scripture passages speak of God's jealousy and anger concerning Israel's adultery both in the Old and New Testament. In light of these references, to think that He doesn't mind mixed authority and relationships with His Beloved Church, would be self-deceiving. If the structure within the Church is not in accordance to His plan and vision, how can it produce His Kingdom purposes?

We can only speculate how this substitution affects the Father, Son and Holy Spirit, but even that amount of speculation can help us realize the scope of the problem.

The Father

From the beginning, Father God has intended for man (male and female), to exist in His presence, at peace with one another and to extend His rulership over the earth, functioning together as a team, unified with Him.

God put the Tree of Life in the center of the garden, because He intended for Adam and Eve to eat of it. He assigned them to a strategic mission on earth and they needed food from that special tree to carry out their assignment. They had been created as tri-fold beings – spirit, soul and body – and God intended for the Tree of Life to feed His supernatural, eternal life to them.

There was also a forbidden tree in the garden. As we know Adam and Eve were banished from Paradise because they disobeyed the Father and ate from it. As a consequence of their choice, He could no longer permit them to eat from the Tree of Life... "...lest (they)...take also of the Tree of Life, and eat and live forever" (Genesis 3:22, NKJV). It would have been a travesty for the power of the eternal life in that tree to be accessed and connected to evil.

This act of independence and rebellion against God separated Adam and Eve from the supernatural fellowship that they previously had with Him. It was now necessary for them to function on physical and soul-driven strength alone. God had to send His Son to restore man back to the divine fellowship which was lost. In John 10:10, God's Word says He came to give us life "more abundantly" (NKJV) and "to the full" (NIV). Christ is now the living Tree of Life, and we must eat of Him. Only Christ's own Body, filled with His supernatural life, can manifest His Kingdom purposes from nation to nation.

Just as God presented the woman Eve to Adam as his bride by forming her out of his body, so He is preparing the Bride for His Son. She similarly is emerging from Christ's own body. Just as Eve was taken from a living being by God's hand, so the Bride of Christ must come forth in the same manner, formed and brought about by God's own hand.

The substitution of the headship of marriage for Christ's headship over the Church wounds God's Father-heart and interferes in all aspects with His purposes: His order of headship has now been altered; the preparation of His family is hindered and there is a tampering with His Son's Bride; His Life - flow is blocked. But most importantly, His authority is not respected and the Church has lost its reverence of Holy God!

The Son

As the first-born Son of the heavenly Father, Jesus is now:

- Head over all the Body of Christ on the earth, as her total source, direction and life.
- The Seed manifesting as multitudes of sons (seeds) of God through Himself, for the Father.
- The betrothed One, covenanted with a Bride being formed for Him.

The substitution also interferes in aspects of His positions, such as King, Lord, Provider, High Priest, and Husband. It wasn't His intent for the Bride, the sons, and the Body to be influenced by other persons. Another is trying to rule over His Bride asking her to submit wrongly to him. John the Baptist foresaw this danger when he said:

> You yourselves can testify that I said, 'I am not the Christ but am sent ahead of Him.' The bride belongs to the bridegroom. The friend who attends the bridegroom waits and listens for him, and is full of joy when he hears the bridegroom's voice. That joy is mine, and it is now complete. He must become greater; I must become less (John 3:28-30, NIV).

When the friend, (another part of His own Body, not her Head) stands wrongly in His place, Christ's righteous jealousy becomes inflamed. The life-seed that has been sown into the Body is being tampered with and altered. He paid for her with His life, and she belongs to Him alone. Only He can work through His Spirit to manifest the fullness of what God has purposed in and through her from the beginning.

The Spirit

He is God's own Spirit, the breath or wind of God's essence. He has eternally been a distinct member of the Godhead. God uses plural language forms to speak of Himself, such as in Genesis when He says He created man in *our* image. Since Pentecost, Holy Spirit has become a divine resident in Christ's Body. His presence and operation are the primary aspects that make Christianity different from the religions of the World. Many in the world relegate Christianity as being just another religion, but Christianity is very different. It is a living relationship with God Almighty, through Holy Spirit's internal presence. Thus there is the need to be born of the Spirit, as Jesus told Nicodemus.

When man acts as Head of the Church, it deteriorates into just another organization and religion. He assumes that Holy Spirit will help him: show up when requested; manifest gifts when they are needed; behave as expected. Man thinks that Holy Spirit should help *him* become an independent son of God, and assist *him* in the preparation of the Bride. This is a manifestation of Satan's prophecy to Eve, ".. and you will be like God, knowing good and evil." (Gen.3:5b, NKJV), and thus, the twisted result that has transpired.

The Church

How has this substitution of headship affected the Church? Instead of being one Body of many members in the way God intended, the Body of Christ is divided and separated into various segments.

External division: There are a vast number of different denominations – Baptist, Lutheran, Pentecostal, Catholic, and Anglican with thousands more unnamed – and many of them have variations and divisions within themselves. The lovely fruit and power of corporate oneness – a sign of Christ's headship – is marred. That wonder and power of oneness was evident in the early Church as described in the New Testament, and we now longingly read about it. Many have tried to re-create New Testament forms hoping to achieve similar results, but the issue is deeper than form.

We teach and preach the Life that the Word speaks of, but see little manifestation of it because of division and disorder within the Body. Only complete connectedness to His headship can reveal His true Body.

Internal division: The Church is divided by the very things which Christ said should not create division: walls of ethno-race, of gender, of economics, of the law, to name a few. The results are multiple:

- The Church cannot fully function as the unified Body that God planned it to be, one through which every member fulfills his purpose in God. Instead it is limited within the order created by man.
- The Church's rightful, shared authority brought to earth by Christ from Heaven is hindered and greatly reduced.
- Instead of experiencing the full mantle of Christ's Body with corporate authority that comes from Christ's full headship, the Church limps along with an inappropriate form of compromised household authority.
- The anointing and power that would reveal Christ's

glory and headship is greatly diminished.
- The Church is limited to a form of godliness without divine power.
- Members within the Church Body are disconnected from one another as they strive within this compromise. Signs of death, weakness and disunity abound. Only Christ's headship in full operation can produce life, authority and unity.

In his book *Manifesting Your Spirit* Graham Cooke describes the problems in churches around the world this way:

> ...[they] are built on a functional paradigm. All the interactions are driven by task, vision, strategy, and purpose. They are geared to doing the most they can in the shortest time possible, with the least amount of resources. Buildings are developed to give people a nice physical environment. Programs exist where everything is done for you. It is a monoculture where we produce clones not disciples. Individuality is not greatly appreciated, and true supernatural spirituality is not encouraged. Everything is planned, logical, and rational, but not spiritual, intuitive, and prophetic.
>
> People are marshaled and taught to be consumers. There is an unwritten code of behavior, assumed rules, and hidden penalties.
>
> Leaders in these places oversee the development of people spiritually but do not allow them to have encounters with God. They do not have the passion or touch that empowers life to flourish in all its forms. In short, it is not lead by the Spirit. It is full of good, not God, ideas. People are leaving there in thousands – not because they have lost faith, but because they need to find it.[1]

Cooke prefaced these comments by saying, "I have been both privileged and dismayed in my experience of churches around the world." [2] (His positive comments are in Chapter 10.)

Finally, we come to ask how men and women of the Church are affected by this substitution. Is it beneficial or detrimental for either gender? For both, the draw to the familiar and to the traditional is very strong. George Otis Jr. describes it this way:

> The gravitational forces associated with tradition, like the vortices of celestial black holes, often appear irresistible. Sociologists attempting to explain this phenomenon, point to strong linkage between tradition and identity. Like it or not we are all part of a tribal continuum, and this continuum largely dictates what we think about ourselves and our world. [3]

The gravitational pull referenced above relates to both our basic gender issues and our familiar church roles. This is often called "the tyranny of the familiar," and it takes the power of God to overcome this strong pull toward traditional roles and ideas. God wants to separate us from the control of these natural inclinations so He can move us into His Kingdom perspectives.

The effect on women

Let us examine the influence of this compromised headship system on women.

Many women seem to flourish under it. They encounter familiar responsibilities here: a family structure, taking care of kids, cleaning up, organizing, providing meals, and generally caring for a place and people.

Women find emotional fulfillment through the love of

God that "has been poured out in (their) hearts" (Romans 5:5, NKJV) because it touches women at their deepest level of need. They are often emotionally hungry and find satisfaction in worship, prayer and service.

Women are created to blossom in their homes under godly headship and they can respond to it even outside of the home. Many Christian women are frustrated with what they perceive as a lack of headship at home and can find a substitute form in the Church where men function as Head. Some women are more submissive to a church leader than to their own husbands and many a husband feels replaced, either by God, or by the Church.

If women seem to be generally doing well, then what is the problem? The problem has to do with the seed of God living within each woman. As she reads the Word and seeks God's will for her life, these familiar responsibilities are not very satisfying. God may want her to be a modern Priscilla, or Lydia, or Miriam, or Deborah, or Mary, but this substitute system does not permit her to function as did the women of the Bible. If she cries out and asks to be like them she risks being labeled un-submissive and is characterized as a trouble-maker. She is often called a "Jezebel".

Some women find an alternative outlet for their gifts and callings. They seek external Christian women's groups or professional opportunities with more liberty to pursue leadership roles.

The effect on men

Though this false substitute system is male - dominated, it does not mean that the men have the advantage. In fact what God has shown me, to my surprise, is that it has hurt men the most.

In the system of household headship there are two basic positions: husband as head, wife as body. When this headship is applied to the Church, the positions for men are limited because there are too few leadership roles compared to the number of available people. To connect to a position, one is required to advance, as in a job situation, with built-in steps to achieve it. This often creates a situation of frustration and competition.

If a man manages to acquire one of these leadership positions, then he can function as a type of head. That may be satisfying and productive to a point. He may even do better at headship in this false church structure than he does at home, because the job description may seem clearer, or the body may be more respectful, thankful, responsive and co-operative.

But what about the volume of men who are not in these primary positions? The rest of the job responsibilities in this system seem womanly or wifely: the need to sit passively while being taught, prayer groups, counseling, or participating in other servant-type activities. Many men seem to drift. They migrate to the back rows, nap, or retreat at home leaving their wives to do the "church thing" with the kids.

Men certainly want more spiritual satisfaction. Some might even be jealous because women seem to get such fulfillment from their involvement. Others may think there is something wrong with them – that they are not spiritual enough. Women can exacerbate that struggle because they want men to be more spiritual at home. Working in the world can seem easier and more productive for most men. There are men who are called primarily to marketplace ministry and they should focus there. The difficulty is for those who can't find any fulfillment in the substitute system.

What, then, is a man called to be, within Christ's Church Body? According to Scripture, he is a member of the Body of Christ and is to be fitted in, and rightly joined to all the other parts under the direction and management of His headship. With Christ as Head of His Body, positions are endless, with each being vitally important to the well-being of the whole. This could mean a man has a primary leadership responsibility, or he is in an essential place in the visible support system or perhaps is in a hidden one. In whatever way he functions, it will always be a vital one because he is a part of the manifestation of Christ's body on earth.

We are fulfilled when we are connected to the Body of Christ and His supernatural life is flowing. Every man, woman and child, is needed to complete the full measure of the Body. We can only find true fulfillment and satisfaction when we function together as a living part of that Body. Most Christians participating in this substitute headship structure have never fully experienced what God intended for the Church Body, nor have they known the satisfaction of fulfilling their part in it.

As we complete our assessment of the effects of this substitution, some things are clearer:

- God never intended for the headship of the home to be substituted for Christ's headship of the Church. Man's headship in the Church has limited both men and women, thereby greatly restricting the glorious, supernatural plans and purposes of the fullness of Christ within His Body.
- Genuine marriage covenant headship is to be honored and respected by the Church, thus releasing the authority vested in a couple to manifest God's Kingdom.

Churches in alignment

Thankfully, some parts of the Body of Christ are not completely governed by this substitution. In certain fellowships, Christ is honored as Head with all parts of the Body equally available to His directive. It is refreshing to participate in these congregations or even to read about them. For example, several internationally known leaders, including Dr. David Yonggi Cho of Korea and Cesar Castellanos of Colombia, say that when they released women and youth into leadership roles, along with an activated congregation, the growth and life in their churches were remarkable. In addition, some amazing house churches are recognized and respected as godly alternatives to the more formal structures.

Christ's headship over the Church is her hope and the source of all the life and power she needs. Her existence and destiny are manifest in and through Him. When the Body of the Church operates as "many members", symmetry and life-flow are experienced.

With proper headship in place the Church is:

- fully alive, "the fullness of Him who fills all in all" (Ephesians 1:23, NKJV);
- functioning in the authority and anointing destined for her;
- graciously moving as a Body, with purpose and unity;
- covered with His Presence and glory;
- armed and dangerous, and
- capable of passion and intimacy.

When Christ, the Head of the Church and the Body are one, the Church can say, "If you have seen me, you have seen my Christ!" No more wrinkles, no more shame, no more defeat! She is full of His powerful love and victory! She knows what she is to be doing because her Head is releasing directions to her. Instead of being stunted in growth, she manifests full development because the life of the Seed is flowing, from His position as Head, through every part of her.

She has a healthy ability to resist "dis-ease," and develops natural, wholesome desires with no substitutes or perversions. I once heard this topic addressed on a women's international conference tape. The speaker discussed the issue of "spiritual homosexuality" and defined it as a preference for intimacy and deep sharing from the heart, primarily with those of one's own gender. Could this be a contributing factor to the proliferation of homosexuality in our culture?

Our enemy is afraid of the glory that God purposed to be released through us as male and female. Power and authority from Him are connected to our humanity and our genders. Just as in the world where sexuality can be altered and neutralized through drastic surgical procedures, so the false religious authority system in the Church can neuter us spiritually, rendering us passive and wrongly submissive.

We need to ask some important questions: How should this Body-life operate? How should we function within Christ's headship? What needs to be done in light of all of this? If this problem is real, and our diagnosis is correct, then there needs to be an appropriate response. We will deal with that response after we examine real Body-life.

Endnotes

1. Graham Cooke, *Manifesting Your Spirit,* Brilliant Book House, 6391 Leisure Town Road, Vacaville, California, 95687. 2008 , Pages 163,167.
2. Ibid. Page 163
3. George Otis Jr., *Twilight Labyrinth,* Chosen Books, PO Box 6287, Grand Rapids, Michigan, 49516. 1997. Page 211.

Chapter 10
WHAT IS REAL BODY-LIFE?

What should life in the Body of Christ be like? How does this "Body-life" work? Does it fit into everyday life? How does it function when we gather, in small or large groups? What would church meetings be like?

God intended that the life in the Body of Christ manifest His attributes and abilities which include His love, versatility and creativeness. The life and authority of Christ our Head, as made evident through Holy Spirit, are as mobile as we are, and can function everywhere.

The main issue is about the freedom of the Head – Christ – to orchestrate the flow of all His spiritual life that He wants to impart through us, anywhere, anytime, and about our obedience in response to His initiation. Jesus and His disciples (Kingdom people in training) carried this life and the manifestation of Holy Spirit's divine presence everywhere they went. The New Testament is full of testimonies of what happened when God's Kingdom touched earth. Jesus spoke again and again about the Kingdom coming to earth. As He spoke, touched and commanded, miracles happened: the blind, the lepers and paraplegics were healed; the dead were raised;

storms were stilled at His voice; the demonic was exposed and eradicated.

These same Kingdom exploits should be the patterns of His Body-life for us today. When God is ruler within us and we co-operate with Him, then His life manifests, individually and corporately, causing His Church to radiate His divine life. Graham Cooke describes healthy churches in this way:

> [They] have these things in common: they allow people to be themselves, and they have characters that are strong, unique, pleasant, yet dangerous to the dark side.
>
> They see themselves as relational communities where family and friendship are signs of the Kingdom as much as wonders and miracles. People have fun and there is lots of laughter – the gentle joshing of people loved by God through people. Individuality and creativity are much prized, and the whole which we are cultivating contains a structure that is friendly, flexible, and inclusive. It is impossible to not see a place where you could connect and enjoy life. Everyone fits in and is empowered to discover their dream and practice their gifting on the people around.
>
> It's a community of worshippers. Believers who experience God. It is a community with many warriors, workers, and skillful practitioners of life and the arts. It is generous, fun loving, hard working, quietly restful, and Presence focused. People are in Christ, learning to be Christ-like. People are allowed to make mistakes and are given permission to grow and develop.[1]

When it is possible to walk with fellowships that function in like manner, then we are Christ's living ambassadors everywhere we are. He wants us to go with Him to work, to play, to fellowship gatherings, to school, and to the grocery store.

We must co-operate with God's purpose in and through us at all times, everywhere. This is especially important for the lost and needy whom we encounter every day. Some of them need prayer or perhaps wisdom; some may need a touch of kindness or a word, and others need a demonstration of the glory of God. The many demands of people may seem endless, but the wondrous possibilities of God's supernatural intervention into these people's lives are beyond human expectations. Every gift or demonstration of Holy Spirit works anywhere that we are.

For those who might find a daily walk such as this, outside their experience, these possibilities could be considered:

Graham Cooke shares about being placed back in the business world for a season. God lead him to conduct business through prophetic revelation, and thus challenged him to negate the usual, known and reasonable, business practices.

Patricia King, on her television show *Extreme Prophetic* relates stories of how God's Kingdom people are lead by Holy Spirit into the streets and byways. They prophesy and interpret dreams, opening a revelation of God's personal love to the lost.

In some nations like Argentina, for example, an actual formal commissioning of Marketplace Ministers takes place on a regular basis. These are committed people who have been trained to bring the Kingdom of God into the business world. At one event I attended, over 300 were commissioned by Ed Silvoso and local leadership. This heart to release the Body into active ministry is now pulsating around the world.

Another type of active Body ministry is a business group called Divine Exchange. They offer Kingdom business services: helping to birth a business, the imparting of a vision for it, or perhaps the need of a transition, and/ or catapulting it beyond any obstacles. The spiritual gifts of intercession and prophecy help to accomplish this work. Many businesses have and continue to experience the blessing of this service.

Our Redeemer-Husband: Our Head

We all have frequent, daily opportunities to impart God's Kingdom as we encounter needy people: a customer at the store in a wheelchair with an obvious need of prayer for healing; one at work who shares their life and opens a door for prayer or godly advice; a prompting of Holy Spirit to draw attention to someone for an encounter or for prayer. The possibilities are endless.

Let's now consider Body-life within Christian fellowship gatherings. These could range from informal get-togethers, to house-church groups, to traditional gatherings in church buildings and everything in between. God's Spirit flows anywhere the Body is gathered corporately. Consider these situations:

A few years ago while I was attending a large Christian conference in an American city, something quite unique occurred. At the first meeting, after a wonderful time of praise and worship, we settled into our seats with anticipation as an internationally known speaker launched into his delivery of God's Word. He spoke for about ten to 15 minutes and then stopped, saying: "There is no anointing on my message." He then activated the Body by directing us to wait upon Holy Spirit, and to come forward to share any revelations we might receive. We prayed for about 15 minutes. He then returned to the microphone and announced that the leaders, with the discernment of the Body, decided that God wanted us to be in intercession for the city. This became the directive for our time together that morning, and a very special prayer work was accomplished.

This is an example of the Head being free to move in a meeting as He wills, disrupting man's agenda if necessary. The speaker was secure enough in God's love, and sensitive enough to respond to the Spirit's directives from within. He did not have to protect his reputation, or prove anything to us. This demonstrates the fruit possible in the Church Body when people depend more on Holy Spirit than on forms or programs. There is no need to perform or pretend. There is no doubt that God is present; everyone knows He is.

Do you think this is just a Charismatic or Pentecostal phenomenon? No, it is not. The life of God flows wherever it is permitted to do so, as the next example illustrates.

I was attending the funeral of a fellow leader and friend. During the service an evangelical pastor was invited to share. He and my friend had been pastors in the same town, but were at odds with one another due to an old war they had inherited. About a year prior to this funeral, they were both diagnosed with terminal cancer. In the ensuing time through various circumstances, they met, resolved their differences, and became Christian brothers regularly visiting and praying for one another. In that time period, they both received prayer for healing at the meetings of a visiting evangelist.

Throughout the ensuing months many things happened with the result that the one speaking to us was now healed and the other was not. He shared that on the morning of the day our friend died, he felt in his heart he was to set aside his busy schedule and go to the hospital to visit our friend. He obeyed Holy Spirit's promptings, and found our friend alone semi-conscious, hovering between life and death. He sat, prayed and read Scripture, believing this would comfort his dying friend. While reading a significant passage, he realized that our friend had departed to be with his Lord.

God, who is such a loving Father, had not wanted His faithful son to die alone, lying on a hospital bed, so He sent another son (Body part) that morning to be His hands and voice. This evangelical pastor was sensitive to God's Spirit and responded appropriately, fulfilling the vital function.

In both these incidences a person made a decision in response to his faith that God was prompting him through the presence of Holy Spirit.

The next illustration demonstrates a corporate response:

123

During special meetings at a host church with many visitors present, a large crowd was on its feet, very involved in worship. A talented worship leader along with musicians on the platform, was successfully leading us into God's presence. At the end of one song some spontaneous worship erupted. Uniquely, it didn't stop and continued for quite some time!

At first the worship leader looked pleased, but soon became frustrated, and attempted to bring the worship back on track with his program. He could not do it because people were functioning in Spirit as a corporate Body. Amazingly the spontaneous worship continued for nearly an hour and swept us all, including the worship leader who finally joined us, into a glorious encounter with God in heavenly worship.

Hopefully these examples help illuminate the concept of real Body-life, both personal and corporate. The issue isn't *what* we are doing, but *who* is really initiating the activity. We, with our western mindset, are so programmed that we have difficulty with spontaneity. We want to know the exact starting time of any activity, how long it will take, and how to fit it into our busy schedules. We feel secure in the comfort of something familiar, understandable, and predictable. We primarily think that God should accommodate us: allow us to shape our Christian lives into our own image of what is "user friendly" and safe. This is not a Kingdom or Body-life mentality.

By God's grace many ministries are speaking the truth in this hour that the Kingdom of God is far greater than anything we can contain, or manage in a Sunday morning or evening service, or at work. Holy Spirit is not confined to our buildings or formal meetings; He is free to work anywhere, anyhow, at any time. It is our responsibility to relinquish control to Him.

Interestingly, He likes doing supernatural things in public. This truth was evident in Jesus' life and continues to be so in the lives of modern day disciples. As long as the Head, Christ, is free to function through His Spirit without restrictions, there is life in His Body.

As the Church moves forward in this century, we face a series of questions that require answers. The primary issues are: Who governs us, Holy Spirit or we ourselves? Do we really know what it's like for Holy Spirit to lead? Which leadership style do we model? Do we teach and train people to walk with Holy Spirit?

Most of us have been raised in traditional church settings: we go to services regularly, especially on Sunday mornings; we learn how to behave in a Christian manner according to Christian principles; we sit quietly in our seats to be fed each week; and we believe God to meet all our needs – even the self-ish ones. This type of training has negated the full governance of Holy Spirit. In fact some of our Christian teaching is more closely related to mysticism rather than to sound biblical doctrine: we use rituals and methods rather than believe in God's ability to supernaturally lead us. We might be afraid of God's authority and power and prefer religious activity, which could seem much safer, especially within our own familiar groups, but when confronted by new and challenging circumstances, we risk the possibility of floundering. Sid Roth makes this strong comment:

> Many churches have evolved into nothing more than religious warehouses filled with people bound for hell. Members are made to feel they are acceptable to God without repentance of sin. Their church experience is as spectators who never fulfill their destinies in God. Tragically, many do not even have a personal relationship with Jesus.
>
> Over the years I begin to see that even some of the better churches are filled with religious tradition. The pastors seem to be more concerned with the offering, announcements, a full sermon, and a timely ending

than with yielding to the leading of the Holy Spirit.[2]

These are firm words, but they are spoken by a spiritual father who loves God's Church and whose purpose is not to condemn but to awaken us, and to make us ask ourselves which system is functioning.

If we want to be of Christ, we must avoid the deception of the Pharisees who were convinced their beliefs concerning God and His Word were absolutely correct. We must humble ourselves and ask God to examine us. As hard as it is, we need to look at ourselves. Here is a check-list of "vital signs" to help us determine how freely Holy Spirit's life flows in our lives and our fellowships:

- Is there an opportunity during a service or meeting for a child to share a vision, (such as of an angel being present)?
- Is the structure of a meeting flexible enough to allow for someone with a "word from the Lord" burning in them, to interrupt existing plans?
- Can we sit and wait on Holy Spirit, or are we pressured by demands of our schedule?
- Do we allow Holy Spirit to lead worship spontaneously through public singing or silence, as He chooses, through whom He chooses, and for as long as He chooses?
- Do people feel released, empowered, and encouraged to bring God's Kingdom with them into every aspect of life? Is the environment changing where they live and work?
- Is Holy Spirit free to say and do what He wants even if He "steps on a few people's toes"?

You may want to add other good questions: How "routinized"

are we? Is most of what we do predictable or Spirit-led?

Being Charismatic or Pentecostal does not exempt us from these dangers. It may even make us more vulnerable because we are convinced that we are free, while actually we can be as "routinized" or more so, than some groups we judge as more traditional.

While Christ lived on earth many obstacles arose that could have restricted Him: people's expectations, the Pharisees with their religious laws and political pressures. They did not sway Him, for He kept His ears and eyes tuned to His Father and operated accordingly. He left clear warnings about two of the primary obstacles He encountered: "And He cautioned them, saying, 'Watch out—beware of the yeast of the Pharisees (*1) and the yeast of Herod' (*2)" (Mark 8:15, NRSV, numbering mine). The references to "yeast" speak of influence and control.

*1 **The law (religious legalism)** is a form of godliness without the power. It compelled the Pharisees to rebuke Jesus for healing on the Sabbath, and even judged Him as evil.
*2 **World systems** control such things as financial structures, social issues, and political systems. Thus we find Judas trying to force Jesus to act politically and take rulership in order to drive the Romans out of Palestine.

This "yeast" is still at work today attempting to control the Church. Our battle is for the very life of God in our lives and fellowships:

> And we have such trust through Christ toward God. Not that we are sufficient of ourselves to think of anything as being from ourselves, but our sufficiency is from God, who also made us sufficient as ministers of the new covenant,

> not of the letter but of the Spirit; for the letter
> kills, but the Spirit gives life (2 Corinthians 3:
> 4-6, NKJV).

This warning is repeated several times throughout the New Testament. It is a life and death battle for a very special prize: the glorious presence of *Elohim*: Father, Son and Holy Spirit. Adam and Eve lost the privilege of that glorious presence, but Christ has removed that separation, and the privilege of God's presence is ours through Jesus Christ. Now God's purpose is fulfilled in forming a living organism that pulsates with His life (a Body rightly joined to Christ her Head). This is Christ's own Body, purposed for His Kingdom work on earth and eternal life with Him.

Adam's body was fashioned by God for a greater purpose than just for himself. God planned to bring forth woman from his flesh. When God formed her, Adam said: "This is now bone of my bones, And flesh of my flesh; She shall be called Woman, Because she was taken out of Man" (Genesis 2:23, NKJV). She had to be "taken out of" him to be fully part of him: *"two being one"* – not two forms of life, but one with two aspects: male and female.

The creation of Eve is a type of God's ultimate vision for His Son's Bride. The Church, the last Adam's Body, is being formed for more than her obvious service on earth, as great as that is. Christ's Bride, a "woman," is to come out of His Body. She must be "bone of [His] bones and flesh of [His] flesh." They must be one.

Some current teachings imply that we already know who constitutes Christ's Bride. That kind of thinking is risky because of our human tendency toward elitism. God knows who the Bride is and will reveal her in His own time.

The structure and functioning of the Church do not depend on our desires. They depend on God and His preferences. Jesus bought and paid for her and she belongs to Him. The various picture-words that He uses to describe her, give us glimmers of His heart toward her: an army; a vineyard; a city; a Bride; an olive tree.

Life in all its forms, spiritual and natural, comes through the union of Head and Body. The Church, only as a living Body connected fully to her Head, can become what God destined her to be.

What then must we do?

Endnotes

1. Graham Cooke, *Manifesting Your Spirit,* Brilliant Book House, 6391 Leisure Town Road, Vacaville, California, 95687, 2008, Page 163
2. Sid Roth, *The Incomplete Church,* Destiny Image Publishers, Inc., PO Box 351, Shippensburg, PA., 17257-0315. 2007, Page 50.

Chapter 11
WHAT MUST WE DO?

I n answering this question, we need to consider a primary issue: the condition of our hearts. We reason with our minds, but we relate with our hearts. There are two hearts involved here, ours and God's.

Our hearts

God knows our hearts and cares how we respond. He processes life relationally and expects us to do the same. It is vitally important that we are open to Him at this point. The mandate to honor Christ as Head of His Church requires His Body to respond in love and submission.

If your heart became engaged while reading this revelation, then you should have little difficulty responding to God now, but if you have only engaged with your mind, the possibility of change is minimal.

God's heart

What about God's heart? We need to care about the passion which God carries in His heart and wants to share with our hearts. He is looking for faithful, passionate family members – sons and daughters who care about His heart.

Greek philosophy and religious teachings want us to think that God is a detached CEO sitting in His office while his servants keep record of our good or bad behavior. Nothing is further from the truth. Jesus made it clear that our heavenly Father personally cares about every aspect of our life here.

The passion of the Church has been greatly diminished by these alterations that man has made within the Church's foundational structure. God wants to "light a fire" within us for He knows what is on the horizon.

The King is coming! Our beloved Redeemer-Husband-King is coming!

Are we ready for Him?

Are our hearts aflame for Him or are we like the ones whom Christ had to rebuke in Revelation 3:16 –19:

> So, because you are lukewarm – neither hot nor cold – I am about to spit you out of my mouth. You say, 'I am rich; I have acquired wealth and do not need a thing.' But you do not realize that you are <u>wretched, pitiful, poor, blind and naked</u>. I counsel you to buy from me gold refined in the fire, so you can become rich; and white clothes to wear, so you can <u>cover your shameful nakedness</u>; and salve to put on your <u>eyes, so you can see</u>. Those whom I love I rebuke and discipline. So be earnest, and repent (NIV, underlining mine).

He gives instructions concerning healing and preparation. The parable of the ten virgins, in Matthew 25: 1-3, is an exhortation for the betrothed one to make herself ready. Not just any preparation will do; she must prepare using what her Bridegroom has given her: the oil of love.

We are being warned of the consequences of neglecting to have a good supply of this precious oil. In his book *Secrets of the Secret Place* Bob Sorge shares about Mike Bickle's perspective on this parable. Bickle says the parable speaks of leaders who primarily seek God for the purpose of ministry, and not because they love Him and want to be with Him. They behave like the virgins who did not have enough oil. Those who primarily seek God relationally are like those who had an abundance of oil. Not only must it be the right "oil," but the oil must be "purchased" for the right reason.

This parable touches the deep issue of our heart's condition. Are we focused on Christ as were the virgins with the extra oil, or are we consumed with too many other things as were the unprepared virgins who got so close but missed out?

In his writings Jim Chosa likens our hearts to a lamp:

> The Gospel, the Cross, first works in our spirit to remove the dead ashes of our life preparing it to be relit by the fire-light of God in Christ. The wick in this instance is the spiritual heart. In Proverbs 20:27, Solomon says: "The spirit of man is the candle of the Lord, searching all the inward parts of the belly". The word "candle" means lamp, which in ancient times would be filled with oil. A wick would be placed in the oil and lit. This wick would burn and provide light and comfort as long as it was in the oil. For many who desire to move forward today, the wick of our spiritual man must be trimmed of all the religious doctrines of the past, which have locked us down in our spirits and prevented us from truly knowing God as He is.[1]

As Jim teaches, the issue is not about our physical heart, but about our spiritual one: in Hebrew *labe,* which means the center of life. The reality of being one with God in heart and mind, through the Spirit of Christ within, is a primary sign that the Body of Christ is functioning through His Headship.

Our only hope of escaping the false authority of human headship in the Church is through the Cross of Christ Jesus, whereby we die in Him to self and He lives in and through us as our Head.

We need God to reveal any involvement that we have in this system. Whether we are five percent or 95 percent guilty of contributing to the problem, we need to repent. We need that revelation *in order* to repent and then we can take the next step of repentance, which is agreeing with God.

One issue that requires repentance is lukewarmness. Frances Frangipane expands on this need in his article, "Those Who Sigh and Moan":

> There is a great tolerance in the church today. Instead of serving the passions of God, we serve a "philosophy" called Christianity. The ability to intellectualize and define right and wrong has masqueraded as obedience. Tolerance and compromise are now esteemed as virtues; to possess strong convictions is to be labeled as extreme. Hear me beloved, God doesn't want us to simply live in the midst of sin; He wants us to sigh and groan over it.[2]

A prayer of repentance

> Forgive us, oh God!
> Forgive us for blindly following the traditions of our fathers, for serving philosophies and principles, instead of Your Spirit. We ask forgiveness for our-

selves and stand in the gap for each generation in Your Church that has followed the ways of the spirit of the world instead of You, Holy Spirit. Forgive them and us for allowing this one, and other substitutions, to enter Your Church.

Forgive us Father, for interfering with Your purposes and plans.

Forgive us Christ Jesus, for touching Your Church/Bride and trying to be her Head in Your place.

Forgive us Holy Spirit for being afraid to give You Your rightful place of authority, and for wanting to be in control ourselves: being like gods. Please hear our prayer and release Your Church from this bondage. We activate the prayer of Paul, our spiritual father in the faith: "I keep asking that the God of our Lord Jesus Christ, the glorious Father, may give you the Spirit of wisdom and revelation, so that you may know Him better. I pray also that the eyes of your heart may be enlightened in order that you may know the hope to which He has called you, the riches of His glorious inheritance in the saints and His incomparable great power for us who believe" (Ephesians1:17-19b, NIV). Amen.

As we are forgiven, let us humble ourselves and ask Christ to establish His headship over us. If He reveals anything that hinders that headship, we must invite Him to remove it, whatever the cost, and to implement every change that is required.

I urge you to ask Him to be jealous concerning this matter over you, your congregation, your ministry, your business, and your home. Better that we fall on the Rock than the Rock falls on us, as it did on the Pharisees. Better that a child leads us, than we leaders be found guilty of usurping our divine Head's place!

Teach us to pray

While repentance is a primary issue with God, our response must go further. Prayer is critical. God talked to Solomon, as a leader, about prayer:

> When I shut up heaven and there is no rain, or command the locusts to devour the land, or send pestilence among My people, if My people who are called by My name will humble themselves, and <u>pray and seek My face</u>, and <u>turn from their wicked ways</u>, then I will hear from heaven, and will forgive their sin and heal their land. Now My eyes will be open and My ears attentive to prayer made in this place. For now I have chosen and sanctified this house, that My name may be there forever; and My eyes and My heart will be there perpetually (1 Chronicles 7:14-16, NKJV, underlining mine).

God has been exhorting His people to seek His face and pray all through the centuries. Christ came to make possible a face to face relationship with the Father which changed prayer forever. A failure to seek God's face primarily results in prayerlessness, a chronic problem especially among leaders. Dennis Wiedrick writes:

> Sometimes as leaders we create a vertical list of priorities to help us determine where best to invest our time. Many and varied are the demands that come to us. Because we are tempted to please man, rather than God, we tend to order our priorities incorrectly.
>
> I knew that I was called to prayer. I just didn't have time. I was too busy doing "the work of the Kingdom"

and prayer just kept sinking lower and lower on my list.

As we steward the pressures of leadership, many times we can feel that by the time we have answered all the phone calls, kept all the appointments, done all the counseling, prepared all the sermons, visited all the shut-ins, preformed all the weddings, ministered to all our families, nurtured all our children, attended all the meetings, read all the books, listened to all the tapes, entertained all the missionaries, equipped all the believers, and taken in all the conferences, solved all the emergencies, in short, became all things to all men, we have no time for prayer. But paraphrasing what one wise brother said, "The enemy does not fear prayerless preaching, prayerless evangelism, prayerless meetings, or prayerless plans, but when the saints get on their knees, he trembles". [3]

Holy Spirit, please teach us to pray! The disciples made this appeal to Jesus while He was with them. They saw what real prayer involved as He spoke with His Father. They knew what they had called prayer, was not what He was doing, and they cried out for help. They saw that it is more than just words, and is part of a relationship with God through Christ; it must originate from His heart and then flow through our hearts. Through Christ's Body, Holy Spirit wants to activate prayers, decrees and the release of the prophetic, greater than our minds can conceive.

Let us humble ourselves and yield to Him. All prayers must be prayed according to His will and purposes: **Thy Kingdom come, Thy will be done on earth as it is in heaven.**

God has eternal objectives that we barely comprehend, but He will bring them to pass whether we co-operate or not. As for me, I want to be part of God's purposes. I am sure you do as well. Our battle is against the enemy's schemes that are working overtime to try to thwart God's purposes through us, Christ's Body. Satan attempted to do that at Calvary, but failed. People, who were present there, co-operated with him and later regretted it. God forbid, we do not want to do the same. May we yield to God and co-operate with our Head, Christ Jesus our Lord.

Rise up!

Our final step is one of action according to Isaiah 60:1-3 (NKJV):

> Arise, shine; For your light has come!
> And the glory of the LORD is risen upon you.
> For behold, the darkness shall cover the earth,
> And deep darkness the people;
> But the Lord will arise over you,
> And His glory will be seen upon you.
> The Gentiles shall come to your light,
> And kings to the brightness of your rising.

Rise up, oh Church of God, oh Body of Christ; be rightly joined to Him, our Head, and also to one another as "many members"!

We, the Church, need to rise up in demonstration of God's life, displaying supernatural love, power and revelation.

This will be evident on three levels:

- **Locally:** Each member of Christ's Body takes his God-ordained place in that body, energizing the whole with life and furthering God's purpose for lives, homes, local fellowships and communities.
- **City-wide:** Each congregation/ministry thinks and functions as a part of the wider Body of Christ

which makes up the Church of a city. Only the city-wide Body can fulfill that city's godly birthright, and truly bring God's Kingdom into every sphere of that city.

- **Nationally and globally:** The body of believers in each nation, and globally, joins together as one Church, becoming the full Body of Christ on the earth.

When we are truly connected to our Head, Christ, personally and corporately, then God can fully accomplish His purposes and release our Husband to finally come and claim us, His Wife. He has prepared everything.

> And behold, I am coming quickly,
> and My reward *is* with Me, to give to every one
> according to his work.
> I am the Alpha and the Omega,
> *the* Beginning and *the* End,
> the First and the Last.
> Blessed *are* those who do His commandments,
> that they may have the right to the
> tree of life, and may enter through the gates into the city.
> But outside *are* dogs and sorcerers and sexually immoral
> and murderers and idolaters, and whoever
> loves and practices a lie.
> "I, Jesus, have sent My angel to testify to you
> these things in the churches.
> I am the Root and the Offspring of David,
> the Bright and Morning Star."
> And the Spirit and the bride say, "Come!"
> And let him who hears say, "Come!"
> And let him who thirsts come.
> Whoever desires, let him take the water of life freely.

Our Redeemer-Husband: Our Head

(Revelation 22:12-17, NKJV)

Endnotes

1. Jim & Faith Chosa, *Thy Kingdom Come Thy Will Be Done In Earth*, Day Chief Ministries, Montana, USA: 2004, Page 14, 15.
2. Frances Frangipane's article "Those Who Sigh and Moan".
3. Dennis Wiedrick, *The Royal Priesthood*, Wiedrick & Associates, Hamilton, Ontario, Canada. 1997, Page 32, 33.

APPENDIX

Vines: HEAD, *Kephale* 2776 besides it's natural significance, it is used figuratively in Rom. 12:20, of heaping coals of fire on the "head" (see coals); in Acts 18:6, "Your blood be upon your own heads," i.e., "your blood-guiltness rest upon your own persons," a mode of expression frequent in the O.T., and perhaps here directly connected to Ezek. 3:18, 20; 33:6, 8; see also Lev. 20:16; 2 Sam. 1:16; 1 Kings 2:37.

Metaphorically, of the authority or direction of God in relation to Christ, of Christ in relation to believing men, of the husband in relation to the wife, 1 Cor. 11:3; of Christ in relation to the Church, Eph. 1:22; 4:15; 5:23; Col. 1:18; 2:19; of Christ in relation to principalities and powers, Col. 2:10. As to 1Cor. 11:10, taken in connection with the context, the word "authority" probably stands, by metonymy for a sign of authority (RV) the angels being witnesses of the preeminent relationship as established by God in the creation of man as just mentioned, with the spiritual significance regarding the position of Christ in relation to the church; cf. Eph. 3:10; it is used of Christ as the foundation of the spiritual building set forth by the Temple, with it's "cornerstone," Matt. 21:42; symbolically also of the imperial rulers of Roman power, as seen in the apocalyptic visions, Rev.13:1, 3;17:3, 7, 9. [1]

Holman: HEAD, Literally, the uppermost part of the body considered to be the seat of life, but not the intellect and figuratively for first, top, or chief. The Jewish notion was that the heart was the center or seat of the intellect. "Head" meant the physical head of a person (Gen. 48:18; Mark 6:24) or of animals, such as a bull's head (Lev. 1:4). It was often used to represent the whole person (Acts 18:6). Achish made David "keeper of mine head," that is his bodyguard (1 Sam. 28:2).

Head" was used frequently to refer to inanimate objects such as the summit of a mountain (Ex. 17:9), or the top of a building (Gen. 11:4). The word "head" often has the meaning of "source" or "beginning," that of rivers (Gen. 2:10), streets (Ezek. 16:25), or of periods of time (Judg. 7:19, translated here as "beginning").

In Psalms 118:22, "head of the corner" (cornerstone) refers metaphorically to a king delivered by God when others had given him up (compare Matt. 21:42; Acts 4:11; 1 Pet. 2:7, where it is used in reference to the rejection of Christ). "Head" designated one in authority in the sense of the foremost person. It can mean leader, chief, or prince (Isa. 9:15), and it can have the idea of first in a series (1 Chron. 12:9). Israel was the "head" (translated "chief") nation, God's firstborn (Jer. 31:7). Damascus was the "head" (capital) of Syria (Isa. 7:8). A husband is the "head of the wife" (Eph. 5:23). [2]

To order additional copies of

Our Redeemer-Husband: Our Head
by PATRICIA A. HUGHES

have your credit card ready and call
USA: (800) 917-BOOK (2665)
Canada: (877) 855-6732

or e-mail
orders@selahbooks.com

or order online at
www.selahbooks.com

or contact
Patricia A. Hughes
Maranatha Apostolic Ministries
PO Box 731, Station B, Sudbury, ON., Canada, P3E 4R6
705-855-0878
www.maranatha-apostolic.com
contact@maranatha-apostolic.com

LaVergne, TN USA
24 August 2010
194347LV00004B/2/P